Dixie
Chicks

Dixie Chicks

DOWN-HOME AND BACKSTAGE

James L. Dickerson

Taylor Trade Publishing
Dallas, Texas

Published by Taylor Publishing Company
1550 West Mockingbird Lane
Dallas, Texas 75235
www.taylorpub.com

Library of Congress Cataloging-in-Publication Data
Dickerson, James.
    Dixie chicks : down-home and backstage / James L. Dickerson.
        p. cm.
    Includes bibliographical references and index.
    Discography: p.
    ISBN 0-87833-189-1 (pbk.)
        1. Dixie Chicks. 2. Country music groups—Biography. I. Title.

ML421.D58 D53 2000
781.642'092'2—dc21
[B]   00-042591

10   9   8   7   6   5   4   3   2   1

Printed in the United States of America

Dedicated to all the Dixie Chicks fans
on the Internet
who helped with this book

CONTENTS

ACKNOWLEDGMENTS

I would like to thank the following people for helping me with this book: Asia Abraham, Cary Banks, Roy Bode, Robert Brooks, Leigh Browning, Al Cooley, RuNell Coons, Ben Dixon, Sarah Godcher, Janelle Hackenbeck, Whitney Israel, Stephen John, Nici Larson, DeAnna Lee, Angie McIsaac, Ken Michaels, Greg Morrow, Vicki Nash, the Public Library of Nashville and Davidson County, Thom Oliphant, Katie Pruett, Jay Rury, Tom Van Schaik, Larry Seyer, David Skepner, Michael Sommermeyer, Danielle Syx, Johnny Thorn, Mac and Laura Lynch Tull, the Jean and Alexander Heard Library at Vanderbilt University, Randy Ricks, and Cynthia Wagner; my agent for this book, Frank Coffey; and my editor at Taylor Publishing, Mike Emmerich.

INTRODUCTION

Martie fiddles, Emily plays banjo and dobro, and Natalie sings
in the voice of a honky-tonk rose who's seen it all but
hasn't ruled out love . . . The Chicks are country's finest
proponents of high-spirited thrills.
Rolling Stone
January 7, 1999

*N*ot since Elvis Presley, Scotty Moore, and Bill Black got together in the 1950s to invent rock 'n' roll, has there come along a musical group with such a compelling story to tell.

If you are among those who consider the Dixie Chicks a female version of Milli Vanilli (a devious concoction put together in the dead of night by cynical music executives) or an accidental collision of ditzy brunettes-turned-blondes out on a musical joy ride (attitudes that have plagued the band for years)—or, better yet, a country version of the Spice Girls—then you are in for a major surprise.

Frankly, when I began work on this book, I did not know everything that was involved with the Dixie Chicks' "overnight" success. Few people outside of Texas could possibly have been aware of more than a few pieces of the story. To discover the true story about the Chicks, I talked to a lot of people. The more I learned about them, the more fascinated I became with their story.

In the beginning, there were four Dixie Chicks—Robin Macy, Laura Lynch, Martie Erwin, and Emily Erwin. The band drew its first breath in 1989, when what we now call alternative country music was nowhere to be seen.

The women had a vision of where they wanted to go with their music, and from the first day they performed on a Dallas street corner in 1989 that vision has been shared by hundreds—and later, thousands—of ordinary Texans.

Over the years, the band changed—Robin left in 1992, and Laura was replaced by Natalie Maines in 1995—but the essence of the Dixie Chicks remained essentially the same, and the band's popularity continued to grow. There is very little difference between a three-person band and a four-person band, except the size of the paycheck each band member takes home; the differences arise in the personalities of the band members.

It took years of hard work for the band to release an album on a major label. The reasons for that are complex. The country music industry—and that includes record label executives, program directors at radio stations, and talent buyers for state fairs—has long harbored hostility toward women entering the industry, especially very attractive women. Most other industries that have discriminated against women have operated in the opposite manner by giving preferences to more attractive women.

Between 1990 and 1995, the Dixie Chicks were considered "too pretty" or "too prissy" or "too off-the-wall" to ever make it in country music. The fact that Emily and Martie were extraordinarily talented instrumentalists didn't seem to matter to the music executives who signed new artists.

The Dixie Chicks owe their success as much to word of mouth among their fans as to the radio program directors who later heralded the group as the newest hit act out of Nashville. They are especially indebted to the Internet for spreading the gospel, for it is there that teenage girls and women in their early twenties exchanged information about the Dixie Chicks and, in essence, created a cultlike following for the group.

Once word got out that I was writing this book, it spread like wildfire over the Internet. The result was that I received much e-mail from Dixie Chicks fans, each telling me about concerts they attended and meetings they had with individual Chicks. I spoke to many of them on the telephone in an effort to more fully understand who they are and what they like about the Chicks. Sometimes I met with them in person. I have used some of their stories in this book.

In addition to the many music awards the Dixie Chicks have won, it is increasingly apparent that they have broken new ground on the Internet by becoming country music's first cyberspace superact. Country music labels have established the obligatory Web sites over the past few years to promote their recording acts, but not until the arrival of the Dixie Chicks did any of them perceive the Internet to be a way of breaking new acts.

The Dixie Chicks have made the record labels more acutely aware of the power of the Internet as a marketing tool. With time, it may just revolutionize the record industry, particularly with the development of more sophisticated sound transfer systems.

To fully appreciate what the Dixie Chicks have accomplished, it is helpful to look at the statistics. Since 1987, the major record companies have released a variety of albums by women in the categories of country, rock, and pop. A number of solo female country artists achieved success, including Tanya Tucker and Patty Loveless. There were also a few successful family duos (the Judds and the Sweethearts of the Rodeo).

Interestingly, only a handful of female country artists made it onto the Top 20 pop charts (which are based on album sales). They include Dolly Parton, Reba McEntire, Trisha Yearwood, Deana Carter, Mary Chapin Carpenter, and, of course, the female country artist who has sold more albums than any other female country singer in history, Shania Twain.

What makes the Dixie Chicks unique is that they are the first female country *band* to succeed on the pop charts. Actually, only one other female band in any category over the past decade has duplicated that feat: the Bangles. (Heart and The Go-Go's made the Top 20, but that was in the 1970s and 1980s.)

It is also useful to compare actual sales. *Wide Open Spaces* sold over four million units its first year of release. That puts the Dixie Chicks in the same sales category with Alanis Morissette for *Jagged Little Pill,* the Cranberries for *No Need to Argue,* and the Beatles' *Live at the BBC.*

Where all this is going is anyone's guess.

On the country side, new female groups such as SheDaisy are leaping onto the wave created by the Dixie Chicks, and, on the pop and rock side, bands such as Luscious Jackson and Hole are witnessing renewed interest in their work, and that has translated into skyrocketing album sales. Hole's frontwoman, glam rocker Courtney Love, was in the spotlight long before the Dixie Chicks spun their golden locks into platinum; but the success of the Chicks has had a noticeable impact on Love's dedication to her music.

Over the years, each of the Dixie Chicks has had other career choices—Emily once toyed with the idea of joining the Air Force to become a fighter pilot—but they stuck with their music because it represented a dream they were not willing to give up. Whatever you think of their music, you've got to admire their gumption.

The Dixie Chicks are three (make that five) very savvy ladies.

Dixie Chicks

THE EARLY BIRDS GET THE CHICKS

1989—1990

When the imposing gray Caprice Classic screeched to a stop at the street corner, some passersby may have thought it odd that the business end of an upright bass would be protruding from the backseat window of the car. But it was the West End of downtown Dallas, Texas, after all—and it was summer and, with the sidewalk filled with vendors and entertainers, no one paid that much attention to the car.

All that changed quickly, when the car doors flung open and four big-haired, knock-dead gorgeous women dressed in cowgirl outfits leaped from the car and unloaded an assortment of musical instruments onto the sidewalk.

There was dark-haired Laura Lynch with her upright bass; sandy-haired Robin Macy with her acoustic guitar; Martie Erwin with her fiddle, blonde hair, and bright, greenish blue eyes; and Emily Erwin, the tallest, youngest, and blondest of the group, with her banjo. The four women (Laura and Robin were thirty-one, Emily was seventeen, and Martie was twenty) made a mad dash for the street corner and—before any of them could lose their nerve—immediately broke into a foot-tapping bluegrass number.

Visually, it was like something out of a Fellini movie. It had a surreal quality. The women wore brightly colored skirts and blouses, cowboy boots, and western-style hats, a throwback to the Roy Rogers and Dale Evans cinematic imagery of the late 1940s and 1950s.

A crowd gathered around the quartet in no time at all. Even without the music, the women would have attracted a crowd: Laura, with her long mane, hair-trigger smile, and exotic beauty; Robin with her clean-cut, schoolmarmish good looks; Martie with her cheery, cheerleader face; and Emily with her finely sculptured facial features.

But, despite their good looks, these women could sing and perform with the best of them. Laura and Robin took turns with the lead vocals, with Martie and Emily pitching in with harmony when needed.

If it was their good looks that stopped traffic, it was the music that kept the crowds standing around for hour after hour. Even if you weren't fans of bluegrass and country swing, you had to appreciate the dazzling musicianship displayed by the sisters.

With her leg cocked to one side, Martie leaned into her fiddle, pushing the music as hard as she could with a series of fingering movements that would later leave the ol' boys of Nashville scratching their heads.

Emily, still too shy to look into the faces of the crowd, played her banjo with a brashness that at times seemed hypnotic; you didn't expect such a timid soul to play with such authority. Young girls like Emily are supposed to aspire to careers as models, not banjo pickers. For the shock value involved, seeing these women perform was analogous to seeing fellow Texan Ross Perot take the stage as a Chippendale dancer.

"People gathered around us and never left," Laura recalled in a 1999 interview. "They'd still be there three or four hours later. We only knew about a dozen songs, so we kept starting at the top of the list again. We thought we had a pretty good collection of songs . . . But the best place to find out what works is on the street.

"We used those opportunities to play in front of people when they didn't have to pay to come see us. We would find things out, like what do you like? What works for you? They would tell us. People are very honest on the street. You get the raw opinion, and you get the truth."

Truthfully, the women were a hit in Dallas from day one. They didn't have a name for the group, for in their haste to learn the music there had been no time to invent one. As the weeks rolled by—and the crowds increased—the difficulty in selecting a name grew.

To understand their dilemma, you have to travel back in time. The year was 1989 and the top country artists were Clint Black, George Strait, and Ricky Skaggs. With the exception of the Judds (Naomi and Wynonna) and Reba McEntire, country music was almost exclusively a male playground. Pop music was more gender friendly, with hits that year by Janet Jackson, Paula Abdul, and Debbie Gibson, but the women on the street corner were cut from a different cloth.

So, how do you find a name for an all-girl group that dresses in retro-cowgirl outfits and plays acoustic bluegrass and western swing with a passion that is usually reserved for men with pot bellies and graying hair? The women didn't seem to fit any existing category—and they knew it.

While they struggled to come up with a suitable name, they continued to perform on Dallas street corners. "Our very first audience members were the other street people, the guys who sell roses and the magician and the guy who does caricatures with charcoal," Laura recalls. "Those three were our first audience members. No one knew who we were. The street people gathered around because we were one of them. Everyone on the street looks after each other. We were like a little club.

"We went down there, thinking, 'Well, let's not open our guitar cases. Let's just see if anyone comes to listen.' When people started giving us tips, we thought, 'Well, why not?' So we opened up the guitar cases, and soon we were taking in three or four hundred dollars in a couple hours' time."

Bolstered by tourists, conventioneers, and men in business suits and women in tailored suits, the "little club" quickly grew into a good-sized crowd, even by Texas standards. "Sometimes they would go to our corner, and they would be waiting for us," Laura says. "We'd pull up and . . . and we'd start pulling out our instruments, all these bodies pouring out like the clowns at a circus tumbling out of a Volkswagen. Out came this big double bass and five guitars and a couple of banjos and a fiddle and lots of hats and whatever stuff we dragged around.

"They'd start making noise before we could get unpacked. We made some of our best friends there on the street. Pretty soon, on some nights we would have four or five hundred people encircling us, watching us and waiting."

Invariably, someone in the crowd shouted out, "What's your name?"

Each time that happened, the women looked at each other and giggled. The notion that four women all dolled up with big hair, heavy makeup, and cowgirl outfits would have no name did seem slightly ludicrous. What were they waiting for? How long did they think they could continue to be anonymous street performers?

Not until they wrangled their first audition for an indoor gig did the women realize they had to have a name. As they were on the way to the audition in Emily's Caprice, a song titled "Dixie Chicken" came on the radio. Recorded in 1973 by Little Feat, the song was still popular in the Southwest and the South.

With its references to Dixie chickens, Tennessee lambs, and the fictitious Commodore Hotel in Memphis, the laid-back, blues-rock song struck a nerve with the women's gritty side. Imaginary lights flashed and buzzers sounded, just like in the cartoons. At last, the women had an identity.

"We couldn't be the Tennessee lambs, so we had to be the Dixie Chickens," Laura says. "By the time we arrived at the audition we were the Dixie Chickens. We got the gig and left to have some business cards made up—you can't be a band without business cards—only when we arrived with our sixty-three dollars, we found that the name 'Dixie Chickens' didn't fit on the card."

The name was too long, so they trimmed it down to Dixie Chicks. "At first, we were hesitant because it was slang and could be construed as derogatory to women," says Laura. "But the letters fit on the card, so we used it."

A decade later, Martie looked back on the group's Southern-fried origins with good humor. "If we had known we were going to get beyond the street corner, we probably would have thought about the name more," she told the *Los Angeles Times*. "But every time we thought about changing it, our fans wouldn't stand for it."

"In the beginning, we got a letter from someone who said, 'Why don't you just call yourselves the Southern White Women?'" Laura says. "Then we got other letters from people who liked the name. It had sass, it had priss and sarcasm, plus it rolled off the tongue really easily. As far as marketing goes, it was brilliant."

Like most other "overnight" pop-culture phenomena, the Dixie Chicks was born of a peculiar mixture of necessity and stubborn blind luck. Add to that a generous portion of girl power, seething with girlish ambition and wild-eyed idealism, and you had the makings of a successful twentieth-century business enterprise.

These Chicks were no man's fools. How they got to that first street corner seems as unlikely as the success that would later make them, with some major personnel changes, into one of the most popular all-female recording groups of all time.

Martie and Emily are most definitely "chicks," but their "Dixie" bloodline is suspect. Born in Pennsylvania (Martie, whose actual name is Martha Eleanor, is from York, and Emily is from Pittsfield), they spent the first few years of their lives north of the Mason–Dixon Line with an older sister, Julia. It was in the 1980s that they relocated to Dallas, Texas, with their parents, Paul and Barbara Erwin, who accepted teaching positions at Greenhill High School, a private school that catered to the city's Baby Boomer offspring.

Martie and Emily were introduced to music at an early age by Barbara, who took them to hear the Dallas Symphony. She bribed them to sit quietly and listen to the music, in the hope that the music would somehow sink into their consciousness. She knew that her rambunctious younger daughters preferred to be outdoors, running up and down the school soccer field, where despite the three-year difference in their ages, both girls played on the same soccer team.

Not content to simply let her daughters absorb the music performed by others, Barbara arranged for them to take music lessons on a variety of instruments, including violin, banjo, and guitar. She used an egg timer to regulate their practice sessions at home. "I'd hear kids outside playing kickball, and I hated that I was inside," Emily told *People* magazine. "Now, of course, I'm grateful for it."

Johnny Thorn, who gave violin lessons to Martie from age eleven to sixteen, remembers that she was a very good student. "It was a pleasure to spend time with her because she had talent," he says. "It was really a fun time because she was [so much] into it. I enjoyed listening to her play."

Usually it was Martie's mother who drove her back and forth to Thorn's home in Garland, a suburb of Dallas, but sometimes it was her father. The difference, recalls Thorn, was that the mother seldom left the car, preferring to wait there for her daughter, but the father often came into the house to talk. He would tell Martie to go to the car, says Thorn, and then he would question the teacher about her progress.

Thorn admits that he never thought Martie would become a country music star. "I knew she had talent, but I never thought she would be where she is today," he says. "I don't mean that in a way that she wasn't talented. It's one of those things you don't hear about happening that much. A lot of them [students] have talent and never get there."

One of the sisters' most embarrassing moments, Martie told *Country Weekly,* was when their mother recruited them to perform for the family's garage sale. To the sisters' horror, they were asked to wear bikinis and roller skates, and to play fiddle and banjo on the street in front of their home to entice would-be customers. Signs all over the neighborhood, proclaimed: "Garage sale and live bluegrass band!"

It's impossible to know whether the sisters learned to perform together as a unit because they were unusually close as siblings or whether they became unusually close because of the many hours they spent together racing the egg timer to escape into the warmth of the sunshine. Regardless, they learned to perform musically as a unit, each complementing the other, each compensating for the other's perceived weaknesses. From day one, the sisters would be the musical strength of the Dixie Chicks.

By the time they were in their early teens, the sisters were accomplished enough to perform with the all-teen bluegrass band, Blue Night Express. With Martie on fiddle and Emily on banjo, the band offered a coltish, generation-x version of traditional bluegrass, but it instilled in the young girls a lifelong appreciation of the music.

During those years, whenever Martie found herself unable to devise an appropriate solo when it was her turn to play, she often turned to Johnny Thorn, her violin teacher. Recalls Thorn: "She'd bring a tape and play it so I could hear it. I would play it for her or put it to music [write it down]. She played by ear, so she could pick it up either way."

By the time the sisters met up with Laura and Robin in 1989, they were old pros—Martie was twenty and Emily was seventeen—but still not certain they wanted to become professional musicians.

A junior at Greenhill High School, Emily had become more interested in academics. She put the same energy into studying that she put into her music. Her goal was to be accepted into the United States Air Force Academy and to qualify as a jet pilot. She was completing all the paperwork when she met Laura and Robin.

Martie had by then put in two years of college—a year at Georgetown College and a year at Southern Methodist University, where she had received a music scholarship. As it turned out, she really wasn't college material. "I wasn't the 'smart' one in the family, so my parents supported me in music," she told *Dallas Life* magazine.

Almost a decade older than Martie and Emily, Robin grew up in Missouri, where she played professionally in a folk duet with her sister until she entered college. As a student, her interests changed, pulling her first into the study of political science and then in the direction of pre-law. However, she eventually settled on math and received a degree that allowed her to work as a teacher.

In 1981, she accepted a position teaching math at St. Mark's School for Boys, a private school in Dallas. It was then that she realized she had not purged her love of music from her system. Robin became active in musical theater in Dallas and then looked around for a musical group to join. Teaching math to reluctant little boys who dreamed of riding wild Texas broncos or playing football for the Dallas Cowboys put food on the table, but she needed something more out of life.

In time, Robin joined a Dallas-based bluegrass band, Danger in the Air, in which she sang and played rhythm guitar. The group was well known by those who liked bluegrass music and consistently made the festival circuit across the country.

Like Martie and Emily, Robin sported a flowing blonde mane, but she was a blonde of a different sort. She was pretty but not glamorous like the sisters. Where Martie and Emily had a wild coltish quality, Robin was more serious and thoughtful. Maybe it was the schoolteacher in her. Or maybe it went back deeper into her old-school Southern roots. "We were different," Laura says of her relationship with Robin. "We were into Maybelline (a popular makeup) and tight jeans, and she was more Earth Mama." To Robin, bluegrass music had a purity to it, a naturalness that transcended musical trend and fashion. Success was measured in terms of the duplication of the spirit of the music, not in dollars and cents or public adoration. To tamper with the music, however innocently, was to defame its history and its mysterious hold on her own heart.

Unlike the other women in the group, Laura was born and raised a Texan, and a proud one at that. The daughter of an Irishman, Jack Lynch, and a Hispanic, Pona Cortez, she grew up on a cattle ranch outside Dell City in western Texas (on the Texas–New Mexico border, about seventy miles from El Paso), thriving on what she recalls as an idyllic childhood.

Music was always a part of her life, but not necessarily the biggest part. She was raised a Catholic, but she eventually drifted away from the organized aspects of the religion and made her own separate peace with God.

Laura displayed at an early age qualities that would stick with her all through life: her independence and her penchant for going into a situation well prepared. On her first day of school, she arrived with a brand-new plaid satchel, into which she had packed everything she thought she would need in class, including the family's oversized Webster's dictionary.

When she entered her home room, she recalls, her teacher was so alarmed by the sight of the tiny child ("I was always small for my age") dragging the heavy satchel behind her that she immediately sent her to the principal's office to have her cargo inspected, presumably for bombs or dangerous weapons.

Laura's last encounter with the principal was while she was in the fourth grade, when she received a spanking for chewing tobacco. Perhaps concluding that her brushes with authority were more trouble than they were worth, Laura channeled her adventuresome energies during the remainder of those early years into 4-H, a youth organization in which she raised lambs for show.

"My nickname was BoPeep because of my lambs," she says. "We were inseparable. They ate Oreos with me by kerosene lantern. I spent all my waking hours with them. They were much bigger than I."

By the time Laura enrolled at the University of Texas in Austin, she was thinking of herself as more of a news anchor than a musician. Outgoing and vivacious, she made friends easily and gravitated to the center of whatever was going on around her. In her junior year at the University of Texas, she was named a Young Ambassador for Texas and was sent on a tour of fifteen countries. Before receiving a degree in speech communications, she also studied for a time in Greece.

Laura's first job out of college was reading the news at an El Paso television station. In 1980 she married a man with whom she had a child, Asia Abraham, the following year. ("I don't even want to give him a name," Laura regrets. "He was a geek, though I hear he's grown up some now.")

By the mid-1980s they had divorced, and Laura, with Asia in tow, moved to Houston, where she took guitar lessons and started hanging out at bluegrass festivals. When she wasn't doing that, she worked as a stockbroker and sold real estate for developer Trammell Crow.

By then, music had a firm hold on her. "I met a lot of people in the music business and started a little band," she says. "It was a lot of fun, creative . . . but no one in it was too serious. We all had good day jobs."

In 1989, Laura landed a gig as a backup singer with Robin's band, Danger in the Air, at a bluegrass festival in Fort Worth. It is not unusual for members of one band to sit in with members of another band; it's almost mandatory for anyone who hopes to make a living in music. Laura didn't know Robin well, but she was happy to pick up a couple of dollars and to do what she loved best—sing before a festive audience.

When the set ended, Laura went out into the audience and sat in a seat next to Martie, whom she had recognized from the stage. They weren't friends yet, but Laura had seen the sisters performing around town. They visited for a while, mostly talking about music.

"She was awesome," Laura says, reflecting a common reaction men and women alike had to both sisters, who by 1989 had become minor legends in the Dallas area. "So much talent, energy, just precious. I thought, 'God, this would be fun.' Robin's band was imploding, my band was falling off. The four of us were left standing, so we looked at one another and said, 'OK, let's do it.'"

Martie and Emily Erwin had additional reasons for wanting to form another band. Their parents had separated and were in the process of getting a divorce. The breakup was hard on them, as it is for all children.

Martie was close to her mother. She told Tammy Noles in a 1993 interview for *Trendsetter* that her mother was her primary mentor: "She's always supported my music and she is who I go to for advice on everything from men to managerial contracts."

In some respects, the sisters were an odd pair. Emily has what is commonly called a lazy eye. Her right eye is off-center and turns slightly inward. She always thought it was a deformity that made her look ugly. In later years she would learn the truth, that many men find women with off-center gazes incredibly sexy, usually without knowing why, but when she was coming of age that was a concept beyond her comprehension.

By the same token, Martie always assumed that Emily's classical facial features made her more attractive to men. What she didn't know in the early years, but almost certainly has learned by now, is that many men find female fiddle players irresistible. Whether it is the rhythmic motion of their arms, as they stroke the strings with a bow, or whether it is the way they seem to caress the instrument with their entire body, it is a movement that men traditionally have found appealing. Veteran fiddle player Laurie Lewis, who has put in close to thirty years on the bluegrass circuit, has noticed the phenomenon, but she has no explanation for it. "You find out, you tell me," she laughs.

Laura describes the sisters as "sexy by accident," and there's truth to that. In the early years of performing—first on the street corners and later in the nightclubs—neither had a clue as to the effect they were having on men in the audience. Of the two, it was Martie who dated more that first couple of years. Emily seemed so painfully shy then, it was hard to imagine her ever going out on a date.

When you added to that equation Laura, who possessed a more fiery sex appeal, and Robin, with her Earth Mother allure, you had a group that would have stopped traffic even without the instruments.

"The sex appeal was never overt," Laura says. "Music was the only thing we were selling. I think most of the men who hit on us [while performing] did it as a casual flirtation, which I think is normal. We never experienced anything bad as far as someone being relentless. We were more the girls-next-door type of people. At some point even the most moron of guys will figure out that, well, this is going nowhere. They don't think we get it and really we do. We just aren't going to go there."

More likely to cause trouble were the male club owners who, over the years, had become accustomed to trading bookings for sexual favors from naive, young female entertainers or, at the other extreme, bullying them out of their performance fees.

One evening, an Austin club owner held the Dixie Chicks up for hours before paying them for a performance. "He said he just wanted to have drinks with us," Laura says. "We said, 'No thanks.' Then he leaves for a half hour, and we go looking for him. When he comes back we're still sitting in his office . . . Finally, I said, 'Look, it's 2:30 in the morning and we have a show tomorrow night in another city and we need to get on the road.'

"I tried to get real specific. Finally, he goes to his safe and, oh, he doesn't remember the combination and he's got to go find it. This went on endlessly. I wanted to thump him on the head and say, 'OK, forget it—keep the money, but we're going to tell the whole world on you.' I finally said, 'If you don't give us our money, I'm going to tell the *Austin Statesman.*'

"Finally, he gets his safe open, leisurely. He takes out an envelope and counts out the cash at a hundred miles an hour, and I couldn't keep up with what he was counting. He flopped it into my hands and left the room.

"Well, I counted it and it was almost three hundred dollars short. I thought, 'Well, what should I do?' I decided to tell him the truth, that it was three hundred dollars short. He said, 'Oh, you want me to believe that, with me out of the room?' It was one of those awful moments. They didn't happen often, but when they did, oh boy!"

In the case of the Austin bar owner, the Chicks were never sure whether he wanted them or their money—or both.

Throughout the summer and into the fall, the Dixie Chicks staked out their musical territory. "Come hear Dallas' new sassy bluegrass quartet . . . every Thursday night at Riscky's Bar-B-Q in the West End," read the flyer, which went on to advertise Dixie Chicks bookings at the Hunt County Fair in Greenville, Texas (east of Dallas), and at the Red River Valley Fair in Paris, Texas (about 100 miles northeast of Dallas).

Also, mentioned in the flyer was a booking at Uncle Calvin's, a church-sponsored coffee house at Northpark Presbyterian Church in Dallas. An afterthought on the flyer, which was handed out on street corners, advised: "Get up and feed the chickens or Pa'll raise the dickens," a not-so-subtle request for donations.

By the first of 1990, bookings were coming in at a steady rate, but with Robin teaching at the boys' school, Martie attending Southern Methodist University, and Emily finishing up her junior year of high school, it was becoming increasingly difficult to gather everyone together to perform.

Come summer, everyone would be free to travel and perform, but hanging on until then was a problem for Laura, the only band member who had quit her job to devote herself full-time to the Dixie Chicks. Her solution was to take a brief leave of absence.

While Robin was grading papers, and Martie and Emily were struggling with school exams, Laura joined a Houston bluegrass band, Texas Rangers, for a brief tour of Japan. "My band members were insane," Laura says. "They were all guys—and they got all sakeed out. But I loved the experience, and I loved the people and the food."

Laura's temporary departure set off warning bells for the other Chicks. They were at a professional crossroads. If they wanted to have an honest-to-goodness band, they would have to make sacrifices. The realization prompted Robin to quit her teaching job at St. Mark's.

Martie's departure at about the same time from Southern Methodist University was not so deliberate. She had entered SMU on a music scholarship, but one of the conditions of the assistance was that she play in a school band or music group. Says Laura, "She was always gigging with us and didn't do that part and lost her music scholarship."

For most of her life Martie had apologized for not being "the smart one," but her association with the Dixie Chicks brought something new into her life: That same fiddle that had been an embarrassment during her childhood, suddenly became the vehicle for her empowerment as a woman.

With Emily, who was approaching her senior year at Greenhill High School, dropping out of school was out of the question. However, she would be free all summer, and the way the girls figured it that would be time enough to know if they had the right stuff to make it as an all-girl band.

"I put a lot of things in my life on hold, willingly, because the band was my first priority," Laura says. "Marketing that band was the only thing I thought of. When I woke up in the morning, I thought about how I could market the band. I knew that was all I brought to the band. I didn't bring great musical prowess. I didn't bring a great, LeAnn Rimes-type voice. I didn't bring a dewy youthful presence. I brought marketing. I knew that if we treated people well enough, they would have us back year after year—and they did!"

There was no denying Laura's emerging marketing genius. The first thing she did in the summer of 1990 was ask someone to design a band logo, a circular drawing of a chicken's profile sandwiched between the words Dixie Chicks. She promptly applied the logo to T-shirts that were sold at every performance. In later years, she would develop a stylish and witty newsletter that hawked their T-shirts, CDs, and cassettes, along with coloring books, posters, and autographed photos.

More important, she taught the other women how to interact with the media and their clients so that they would be rehired. The shy sisters only wanted to perform; they didn't want to talk about their music or socialize with the people who were paying them to perform. Robin was by no means shy, but she often seemed uncomfortable talking about their music from a marketing perspective. When the women did interviews, particularly those in which salesmanship was the goal, they depended on Laura to do most of the talking.

However strong Laura's marketing and sales abilities, it was her crystal-clear voice that turned heads whenever her turn came to sing lead. Where Robin's voice had precision and clarity, all essential for bluegrass, Laura's voice had soul and warmth and, perhaps most important, it was accessible to the people standing in front of the stage.

Throughout the summer of 1990, the Dixie Chicks performed anywhere and everywhere. One of their first big bookings was on August 12 at an outdoor concert in Plano, Texas, a suburb of Dallas. It was one of those relaxed, family affairs where music lovers braved the relentless Texas heat and sat stoically on folding chairs, while children ran back and forth in front of the stage, squealing and dancing to the music.

The Chicks wore cowboy boots and white jeans, except for Emily who showed off her long legs in a short, white skirt. They also wore their newly designed Dixie Chicks T-shirts, which were white with the red, black, and yellow logo on the front and a sassy message on the back. Only Laura wore a cowboy hat.

As they faced the audience, it was Martie on the right with her fiddle, Robin with her acoustic guitar, Laura with her stand-up bass, and, on the far left, Emily with her banjo. Robin and Laura took turns with lead vocals, but it was Robin who did most of the talking and who seemed to consider herself the star of the show. Martie and Emily helped with background vocals whenever they were needed.

Musically, Martie and Emily dominated every song, playing off each other with an energy that, once begun, seemed oddly self-sustaining. Providing the rhythm was Robin on guitar and Laura on bass. Laura laid down a surprisingly solid floor upon which the sisters romped with high-spirited abandon.

For an acoustic version of Sam Cooke's rhythm and blues hit, "Bring It on Home to Me," Laura gave her bass to Emily and harmonized with Robin and Martie. Embracing the bass as if it were a barely manageable dancing bear, Emily provided the only instrumentation for the song.

Seemingly horrified at being the only person playing an instrument, shy Emily never once looked out at the audience. The audience seemed surprised to hear the rhythm and blues song, but applauded all the same. For the next song, the Chicks reverted to a more traditional country offering.

"The next number we're going to do, it's only appropriate that an all-girl band do a song that was the first gold record ever done by a woman—and it was back in 1932," said Robin as the applause died down. "The gal's name was Rubye Blevins, but most people know her as Patsy Montana. If your name was Rubye Blevins and you became a big star, wouldn't you want to change it? She was probably best known for her yodeling techniques—and the song is called, 'I Want to Be a Cowboy's Sweetheart.'"

Laura sang lead on this one, yodeling as she thumped her bass in time with the music (she had learned how to yodel by listening to the soundtrack from *The Sound of Music*). When the song came to the bridge, Emily tore loose with a banjo solo that momentarily stunned the audience.

When the song ended, a female mistress of ceremonies, perhaps sensing that the group had just turned the corner with the audience, jumped up on the stage and said, "Aren't they just a knockout?" The emcee then asked for donations for the band. "The kids will be coming around with their hats during the next song."

After another number—Robin sang lead on "Little Willie"—the women staged an impromptu fashion show to display their new T-shirts. Announced Robin: "Yours for just fourteen dollars at the T-shirt stand."

Each girl, with the exception of Emily, who seemed mortified by the exhibitionism of her musical sisters, strode to the center of the stage, sashayed around so that her back was facing the audience, and lifted her hair up over her neck so that the message on the back of the T-shirt could be read by the audience.

"Thank Heavens for Dale Evans," said Laura, quoting from the imprint on the back of Robin's shirt, "which, by the way, is going to be the title of our new album coming out in the wintertime."

Actually, Laura was getting ahead of herself. The song, which had been written by Martie, Robin, and Lisa Brandenburg, seemed a natural for the title of the women's first album, but work on the album would not begin until late in the year, and the CD would not be released until the following year.

When it was Laura's turn to model her T-shirt at the Plano concert (the modeling sessions later became a routine feature of their shows), Emily spoke boldly into the microphone (it was the first and only time she would speak during the entire concert): "The rooster crows, but the hen delivers," she said, reading the line from the back of Laura's shirt. Emily seemed taken aback by the sound of her own voice.

Then it was Martie's turn as she moved center stage and whirled to face the band. Lifting her long hair up past the nape of her neck, she glanced flirtatiously back over her shoulder at the audience (the way the girls do in men's magazines when they're striking "the" pose). The message on her shirt: "Keep on Clucking!"

To this day, Laura swears that Martie and Emily didn't have a clue about how men were reacting to them—and maybe they didn't—but it was certainly a sight to behold.

Throughout the thirty-minute concert, Robin seemed mildly irritated and seldom made eye contact with the other women. You got the feeling that she did not approve of the T-shirt extravaganza and seemed threatened, musically at least, by the sisters' sexuality. Standing between Robin and Emily, Laura smiled at Robin often, in an obvious attempt to draw her into the circle, but Robin was generally unresponsive. By contrast, Laura and Emily exchanged glances often during the concert, showing a genuine rapport.

At the other end of the stage, Martie seemed in her own private world. She tried to hide behind an elevated speaker whenever possible, but occasionally she stepped forward to do something unexpected, such as when she used her bow to flip the pages of the song book that lay on the floor in front of Robin and Laura.

The women received a request for "Rocky Top," but decided to do "Martie's Original Waltz" instead. "Martie wrote this waltz," explained Laura, taking the microphone. "It's only a couple of weeks old, but we sure like it. We're already getting a lot of requests for it. I hope you enjoy it."

Laura provided the lead vocal, with Robin, Martie, and Emily joining in for the harmony parts. As they did the song, a little girl ran up to the front of the stage, sat on the edge, and looked with admiration at Laura as she sang. Other little girls with pony tails and bows in their hair flew to the stage like bugs to a bright light.

Toward the end of the concert, Robin announced that they had purchased a used van the day before. "We're excited about this," she said. "We'll be able to spread out a little more and maybe go all the way to San Antonio. When we first got together last summer, this band started off to be sort of a frivolous, free-for-all thing. Emily came over to pick out a dog, and I got a band out of the deal. Now Laura and I have quit our jobs to do this full time. So, if any of you out there are record executives . . ."

Robin's voice trailed off as she pointed to a man in the audience. "Are you a record producer?" she asked. When the answer came back "no," she continued: "I'm serious folks, as serious as a heart attack."

When it became apparent that there would be no line of record producers forming offstage, the Chicks made one last plea for donations, as they pointed out a giant, ceramic chicken that roosted on the grass in front of the stage, its hollowed-out back soliciting dimes, quarters, dollar bills—anything!

THANK HEAVENS FOR DALE EVANS

1991

Every time the Dixie Chicks performed before a live audience, they did so with a belief that there was a Knight in Shining Armor sitting in the front row who would sign them to a recording contract and make all their career dreams come true.

What they didn't know then was that Nashville recording executives seldom leave the air-conditioned comfort of their high-gloss Music Row offices. They spend much of their time listening to tapes that have been sent to them by producers, managers, and industry insiders they trust. Hopeful thinking by the Chicks set them up for more than one professional disappointment.

"We didn't know how record producers acted," Laura Lynch related in a 1999 interview. "In the early days, these guys would come up to us and say, 'I'm from Atlantic Records [or wherever], and I'm real interested in talking to you about your career. If we could get together after the show . . .' They'd be real smooth and we'd all look at each other, like 'yippee!' So we'd go out with a complete stranger, whomever gave us a card, and we'd find ourselves having tacos at midnight with him. I can't tell you how many tacos at midnight we had—and they weren't record people!"

Slowly, it dawned on the Chicks that they would have to record a demo tape in order to attract record executives to their concerts. With the songs already chosen, now "all" they had to do was raise the money to pay for the recording sessions.

In the summer of 1991, the band traveled to Nashville for the first time, where they performed at the Society for the Preservation of Bluegrass Music of America Convention. Attending the convention was sixteen-year-old Danielle Syx of Alabama, who, like Martie and Emily, had horrified her peers by playing acoustic bass in a bluegrass band that performed in many of the same Texas fairs and festivals frequented by the Dixie Chicks. In a scenario that would be repeated with young girls over and over again, Syx felt an instant bond with the Chicks. There was something about them that helped her define herself as a female.

At the Nashville festival, Syx was delighted when she ran into the Chicks in a backstage hallway. Irrepressible and totally in character, the Chicks were jamming, putting as much enthusiasm into their playing in the hallway as they did on stage.

"I went back in and got my bass and went out into the hallway and jammed with them," Syx says. "I don't think they had been together all that long, but they were real good. I remember Emily, especially. She was really good. She was just a year or two older than I was, and she was so fluent on the banjo. Most kids that age would have had to practice all the time to be that fluent. Martie was good, too. I remember thinking that weekend that if it were possible to hit it big in bluegrass, the Dixie Chicks would. Seeing them like that, and struggling, just made me like them even more."

By the end of the summer and into the fall of 1990, the Dixie Chicks had become favorites of the movers and shakers of Texas society. They performed at private parties and picnics, which by the Lone Star State's standards, were invariably huge social functions.

"We played the same people's Christmas parties, the same festivals," Laura says. "That's how we built our base. We treated the people who bought us great. We wanted to be so easy that when they said, 'Who are we going to get?' they would say, 'Get the Chicks because they have their own sound system and they won't swear or get drunk. Nobody will be a jerk and they will be nice to all our customers' or whoever the party was for."

Joining the ranks of hard-core Dixie Chicks fans were billionaire Ross Perot, Lady Bird Johnson, and United States Senator John Tower's entire family, especially his married daughter, Penny Cook. All hired the Chicks for their private parties, and all seemed eager to spread the gospel of all-girl bluegrass music. The only dark cloud hanging over the girls was their inability to interest a major record label in their music.

**Natalie Maines in cheerleader costume
in this photo from her freshman year at
O. L. Slayton Junior High School,
Lubbock, Texas, 1990.**
Courtesy of Seth Poppel Yearbook Archives/ Hendrie
Photography

***Martie Erwin practices with her
violin at about age four.***
Courtesy of Seth Poppel Yearbook Archives

Emily Erwin in her senior year at Greenhill High School, Dallas, Texas, 1991.
Courtesy of Seth Poppel
Yearbook Archives

Natalie in her junior year at Lubbock High School, 1992.
Courtesy of Seth Poppel
Yearbook Archives

Martie, right, playing soccer during her sophomore year at Greenhill High School, Dallas, 1986.

Courtesy of Seth Poppel Yearbook Archives

The Greenhill High School girls soccer team. Martie is sixth from the left on the back row; Emily is second from the left on the same row.

Courtesy of Seth Poppel Yearbook Archives

Natalie with her high school performance group, "Western Union," during her sophomore year at Lubbock High School, 1991. Natalie is second from the right on the second row.

Courtesy of Seth Poppel Yearbook Archives

Chicks in concert at Samuel Farms, Plano, Texas, 1989. Left to right, Martie, Robin, Laura, and Emily.
Courtesy of the author

Laura in the first grade.
Courtesy of the author

Emily in the studio, 1990.
Courtesy of the author

Emily behind the wheel of the van.
Courtesy of the author

Martie with mandolin.
Courtesy of the author

Merle Haggard gives Dixie Chicks a laugh.
Courtesy of the author

Emily before a performance, early 1990s.
Courtesy of the author

Emily waiting to go on stage.
Courtesy of the author

Laura with her upright bass, July 1990.
Courtesy of the author

**Maines Brothers Band, 1986. Lloyd
Maines is on the far left.**
Copyright © Alan L. Mayor

Chicks take a lunch break on the road, left to right,
Emily, Martie, and Laura.
Courtesy of the author

Martie and Laura rehearse at home.
Courtesy of the author

Martie serenades Laura and Emily at home rehearsal.

Courtesy of the author

Dixie Chicks meet Loretta Lynn.

Courtesy of the author

Dixie Chicks with Al Gore III at President Bill Clinton's inaugural ball. Left to right, Martie, Al Gore III, Laura, and Emily.
Courtesy of the author

Dixie Chicks with Ty Herndon at Mid-State Fair in Paso Robles, California.
Courtesy of the author

Emily with Ross Perot.
Courtesy of the author

That fall, when it appeared their dreams of becoming recording artists would never be realized, a miracle occurred. Penny Cook arrived at Laura's house unannounced. "OK, what do you need?" she asked Laura. "You've got to make a record so that we can hear you when we can't see you."

Stunned, Laura said, "I think it would cost about ten thousand dollars."

Without saying another word, Penny Cook wrote out a personal check to the Dixie Chicks for ten thousand dollars.

"Good luck," she said. "Just pay it back when you can."

For several months in 1991, the band had been toting around the songs they wanted to record, polishing them each time they performed before a live audience, so all that remained was to book the studio time and to make a deal with a manufacturer and distributor. For the former they chose Sumet Bernet Studio in Dallas, where an Englishman, Philip Barrett, worked as an engineer. For the latter, they selected Crystal Clear Sound, a Dallas-based company that agreed to take the master tapes generated at the studio to manufacture the CDs and then to use its in-house distribution network to put the CDs in retail stores. They booked studio time for September and October 1990.

"We had to be skimpy on studio time, so we gathered around the microphones and played the songs live," says Laura. "If we all ended the song at the same time, we'd say, 'That's a keeper' and then move on to the next song. We didn't do any dubbing or any of that rigamarole. We did it the way that was the most efficient and economical."

The album they recorded at Sumet Bernet Studio, *Thank Heavens for Dale Evans,* contained fourteen songs that were recorded live, the way Scotty, Bill, and Elvis had done it in Memphis back in the 1950s and the way Patsy Montana and Bill Monroe had done it even earlier than that.

Robin sang most of the lead vocals, but Laura sang lead on several of the songs. When the two women sang together, it produced a sound that was markedly different than the sound either produced when they sang alone (the sound was different in the way that the sounds from a trumpet and a clarinet are different when combined).

Even so, the real stars of that first album were Martie and Emily. Martie's fiddling was energized, and Emily's banjo picking was the equal to any coming out of Nashville. (Was she really only seventeen and a senior in high school?)

Thank Heavens for Dale Evans proved to be a remarkable album in many respects, but its content and style could not possibly have been further removed from the Nashville sound of the day—and if you wanted to make it in country music, there was no other place to go.

The problem, as far as the Dixie Chicks were concerned, was that Nashville music executives had tired of the bluegrass sounds of Ricky Skaggs and others in the mid- to late-1980s and were eager to sign recording acts that had a more cutting-edge guitar sound. The Kentucky Headhunters, with their slashing guitar work and rock 'n' roll personas, were one of the beneficiaries of that mentality.

Thank Heavens for Dale Evans, whose cover featured a group photograph of the women in old-time western wear with Dale Evans (courtesy of the magic of a clever art director) standing proudly between Laura and Martie, played to the strengths of the Dixie Chicks fan base in Texas. However, it never had a chance of attracting the attention of a major Music City label. That is not to say that the record executives of 1991 were right—if the truth be known, the album would probably have done well in a national market. (During the late 1980s the author owned a one-hundred-station country music radio syndication, and judging by the feedback received from program directors as the new decade dawned, the album would have had a shot at major air play; certainly, the album would have been featured on this syndication.) But right or wrong the Nashville executives were calling the shots.

In the early 1990s, only two artists and repertoire executives in Nashville were female: Margie Hunt at CBS Records, which would soon be purchased by Sony, and Martha Sharp at Warner. Unfortunately, both women were more interested in finding mainstream male talent than in nurturing female talent.

The liner notes of *Thank Heavens for Dale Evans* featured a photograph of Laura whirling her then-nine-year-old daughter, Asia Abraham, about in a circle that sent her retro-cowgirl skirt billowing out. Asia held on for dear life, her hand pressed down on top of her pint-sized cowgirl hat.

Asia was so proud of her mother's CD that she took it to school for show-and-tell. "No one else's mom had a CD," Asia said in an interview. "We played the CD and everyone liked it. They'd say, 'Oh, Asia's mom is so cool, she's in a band.' When my mom came to town she would yodel for my class. Now I would be so embarrassed to have that done. But

THANK HEAVENS FOR DALE EVANS

she would do it at the lunch table. My friends would say, 'Oh, that's so cool. Will you teach me to do it?' "

Asia laughs when she thinks about it today: "I don't think any of them had ever heard yodeling."

Thank Heavens for Dale Evans was released in early spring 1991. In the first few weeks of the album's release more than twelve thousand CDs were sold. Some of the sales were derived from area record stores, but most were sold at Dixie Chicks performances. The group had acquired an almost cultlike following of young women who regarded them as role models and of men of all ages who appreciated their music.

One early fan was Jay Rury, the owner of the Jay Rury Violin Shop in Dallas. He first heard about the Chicks when their soundman, Jeff Humphrey (who had come aboard earlier that year), brought Laura's bass and Martie's fiddle bows in for repairs.

As word of mouth brought him more news about the band, Rury decided that if he were going to maintain their instruments he needed to see them perform. Musicians, especially violinists, play their instruments in a variety of styles, some more harmful to the instruments than others, so it is helpful to someone who repairs the instruments to know how roughly the musicians use the instruments when performing.

"The first time I saw them perform was at Trinity Presbyterian Church," Rury says. "It was pretty soon after the release of *Thank Heavens for Dale Evans*. I liked them very much. Actually, I fell in love with them. Their music was honest and fresh. I'm an old folkie, and I like bluegrass. They had this retro-cowgirl kitsch about them, and I thought they were great."

After the church performances, which also featured poetry readings from members of the congregation, the Chicks joined the audience for cake and cookies in the back room. "You could meet the gals. It was very close, very nice."

After meeting Jay, the girls started bringing their instruments into his shop themselves. "I always enjoyed talking to them when they came in," he says. "Laura would come in with her bass, but it was Martie who came in the most [because Rury specialized in repairing violins]. She was always real nice. She would come in sweats and T-shirt on her way back from the gym, and that was always interesting."

Martie played a rather old generic German violin, says Jay, "nothing particularly special." Once a patron came into the shop with a violin he had purchased in Fort Worth. The instrument had supposedly been used in the Bob Wills band, a legendary Texas bluegrass group of the 1930s and 1940s. "We worked with it for quite some time [trying] to get it to her liking, but she never did like the violin. It was never the sound she wanted."

Thank Heavens for Dale Evans brought the Chicks new hope, but the release of the album was marred by the news that Senator John Tower had been killed in a plane crash. Penny Cook was the Chicks' guardian angel, and her loss of her father was felt by all of the women. The good news was that the album sold so well they were able to repay, within a few months, the money Cook had loaned them.

Nashville record executives, fearful of bucking the Garth Brooks tidal wave, may have been determined to ignore the album, but the media liked it. The Chicks were interviewed frequently on local television and radio. Nationally, they picked up much needed exposure by performing on Garrison Keillor's *A Prairie Home Companion,* and the radio show hosted by the Riders of the Sky.

When *60 Minutes* went to Texas to do a piece on Governor Ann Richards, the Dixie Chicks managed to get some air time when they were shown performing at a function Richards was attending. They were asked to do a thirty-second national television commercial for Mc-Donald's barbecue products, and one of their songs, "I Want to Be a Cowboy's Sweetheart," was used as background music for the popular television show, *Northern Exposure.*

In the fall of 1991, the women performed with Bo Diddley at a concert in Irving, a suburb of Dallas. The newspaper headline the following day read, "Diddley and the Chicks ROCK Irving." Kidd Kraddick, an on-air personality on Dallas radio station KEGL-FM, said the Dixie Chicks were "like the Lennon Sisters on acid."

That year, 1991, the *Dallas Observer* presented the Chicks with its music award for best country and western band of the year. That summer and into the fall, the women went on the road, bouncing back and forth between the east coast and Texas, in their trusty blue van.

One of the highlights of those weeks, they reported in the newsletter they began sending out that year, was picking up a hitchhiker named Emmylou Harris, who desperately needed a lift to her next gig. The country music legend repaid the favor by singing their praises to *Dallas Life* magazine: "I think the Dixie Chicks are great. . . . Their music is good and refreshing. I think it would be wonderful to hear them on the radio."

In mid-June 1991 the Dixie Chicks went to Washington, D.C., to give two afternoon performances at the Texas Heritage Festival at the Kennedy Center. Since that was as close as they had ever come to New York City, they thought it would be a shame not to explore the Big Apple, so they bought plane tickets to New York.

Unfortunately, they missed the flight. With two days to kill—their next performance was at the Birchmere in Alexandria, Virginia—they purchased train tickets to New York and piled into the Amtrak coach with their violin, guitars, banjo, Laura's bass, and their combination sound man/road manager, Jeff Humphrey. Just a bunch of girls, plus one, out on the town.

Seated in the coach behind the dining car with a group of Penn State students, they broke out their musical instruments and played every train song they could think of—and a few they probably made up. The Penn State students clapped and hooted and egged the girls on. In between songs, Laura strolled up and down the aisle hawking Dixie Chicks products. She explained to the passengers that their first CD had gone "aluminum."

No sooner did they get off the train at Grand Central Station, than they found Columbus Circle and set up on a street corner to do their act. Although they were probably dressed differently than most New Yorkers were accustomed to seeing—brightly colored cowgirl outfits, complete with boots and western hats—the city slickers accepted them as just another struggling street act and quickly filled their opened instrument cases with one dollar bills.

They took in enough tips to feel confident they could pay for a room at the Rockefeller Hilton. Of course, they couldn't afford rooms for everyone.

The best way to handle it, they decided, would be for Jeff and one of the girls to check in as a couple. Once they had the room, they could sneak the other girls (along with all their instruments) into the hotel one at a time.

"We were all in one suite," recalls Laura. "We pulled this big, king-sized mattress off the springs so that we would have double the sleeping space."

Back out on the street again, they set up in Washington Square and performed just about every song they knew as their instrument cases again filled with money. Someone in the group, probably Laura, decided that things were going so well they should take a stab at the big time and get a booking on David Letterman's NBC late night show.

There was no point in calling to ask for an audition, they knew that much about the way things worked in New York, so they decided to go for it Texas-style. The Lennon Sisters on acid would not be too far off the mark, especially if you pictured *Thelma & Louise* as two of the sisters. Wearing their colorful retro-cowgirl outfits, they rushed into the main lobby and hurriedly set up near the elevator.

Before the security guard could ask them to leave, they kicked off Sam Cooke's "Bring It on Home to Me," a song they felt the female guard would relate to. Recalls Laura, "We played our hearts out for that security guard. She was a darling lady."

One can only guess what the security guard thought when confronted with four white girls from Texas, dressed in cowgirl outfits—clothes one unhappy newspaper critic once called "Frederick's of Cheyenne"—singing a song made famous by the crown prince of rhythm and blues.

Whatever the guard thought, she handled the Chicks with kid gloves.

"That's real nice, girls, but that's not how you get on the show," she told them, adding with uncharacteristic Big Apple kindness: "But I really enjoyed the music."

Undeterred, the Chicks kept playing.

"We thought, 'OK, if we can just keep playing maybe a staffer for Letterman will get off the elevator,'" said Laura. "We played everything we could think of, ten or eleven songs. We kept playing until we pooped out, and then we were escorted out the door. They said, enough was enough. So we never got to be on the show."

When the time came to check out of the Hilton, they exited as they had entered, one at a time, with Jeff and one of the girls in charge of the official checkout.

"We paid our hotel bill in ones, fives and tens, our street tips, this big pile of money," recalls Laura. "The girl at the counter was onto us, but she liked us a lot. Anyway, she let it slide and got a big kick out of the whole thing."

While the Dixie Chicks had not taken New York City by storm, they certainly left an indelible impression on some of that city's residents.

They rode the train back to Washington, D.C., then piled into their van for a string of one-nighters in Virginia and other states following this schedule:

- June 17—the Birchmere in Alexandria, Virginia
- June 19—Telluride Bluegrass Festival, Colorado
- June 25—concert at unknown location
- June 26—Meatball reunion at Joey Tomatoe's in Dallas
- July 4th—Freedom Fest at Cotton Bowl Plaza, Dallas, with Bruce Hornsby, Cheap Trick, Styx, and Alan Jackson
- July 5—Del Lago Resort, Montgomery, Texas, where they shared the bill with Asleep at the Wheel
- July 6—the Mucky Duck in Houston

The pace was hectic and the summer heat bore down on them every step of the way. "It would be a hundred degrees with makeup melting down our faces," Martie told *People* magazine. "And there's one of us in each seat trying to pull on our little cowgirl suits and boots. Ugh!"

The Chicks did not always know where they were booked. A call would come in. Someone would ask to book the band—and the girls would say, what time do you want us to be there? They couldn't investigate every venue that wanted to book them.

"We took any gigs that came our way," Laura says. "Only once did we back out of one, and it was at a Harley bar. They booked us to start at eleven P.M., and we thought, 'Gosh that's late,' so we called. Some gruff guy said there was no opening act. We were it. He said the bar didn't open until ten P.M., He sounded so crusted we found out where the bar was and found out it was a really rough place we didn't need to go. I'm sure it would have turned out fine, but it seemed strange. People at that hour don't really know what they're hearing."

Try as they might, the Chicks still could not entice Nashville record executives to attend their performances. *Thank Heavens for Dale Evans* had done no good whatsoever in attracting the executives. The girls were not even close to cracking the Music City wall.

Even without the backing of a major label, the Dixie Chicks quickly became one of the most successful bands in the South. They weren't ready to tackle another album yet (albums were expensive to produce and required them to cancel performance bookings), but they started thinking about it. The more they talked, the more the differences among the women began to take shape.

Robin, at age thirty-three, viewed herself as the lead singer for the group (how the other women felt about that is known only to them), and she was strictly old-school when it came to bluegrass. There was nothing about the group she wanted to change. Martie, at age twenty-two, and Emily, at age nineteen, didn't have an opinion at that point. They had the fire of youth in them, and they wanted to push the pedal to the metal.

As the marketing person, the one who had the most contact with the public, Laura, at age thirty-three, was beginning to see the limitations of staying in the narrow groove where all bluegrass performers find themselves. Bluegrass musicians play only bluegrass and do not venture into jazz, rock 'n' roll, or pop music. Like the sisters, Laura was not certain exactly what she wanted from the group. Mainly, she just wanted it to succeed.

It was at this point that Tom Van Schaik entered the picture. A drummer who had been performing around Dallas with various groups, he came across a photograph of the Dixie Chicks in a Dallas newspaper. He recognized Robin Macy, with whom he had once done some musical theater in Dallas. (She had a stage role in the production, and he played in the pit orchestra.) Curious about the Dixie Chicks, he stopped by Joey Tomatoe's (a Dallas nightclub) one night while they were performing.

"There was a line out the door," he remembers. "It was just the four girls playing bluegrass and western swing. I thought it was really cool. I went up and said hello to Robin and introduced myself to the other girls and gave them a business card. I told them that if they ever wanted to put drums on anything they recorded to just give me a call."

A few weeks later, Laura called Tom and told him they were going to record a Christmas song to be released as a single. She asked if he would be available for the session. (Recording a single cost only a fraction of recording an album and could be accomplished in two days.)

On October 9 and 10, 1991, they met at Sumet Bernet Studio in Dallas, where they had arranged for well-regarded independent producer Larry Seyer to supervise production of a six-song demo tape and two songs for the Christmas single. The Dixie Chicks was a studio owner and producer's dream, for when they showed up for a recording session, they paid cash in advance.

Seyer had met Robin in the late 1980s when he produced several songs for Danger in the Air. In what apparently was a compromise be-tween the bluegrass purists and the new-wavers in the group, the demo was recorded without drums, which bluegrass musicians consider inap-propriate for their music.

For the two Christmas tunes—"Christmas Swing," written and arranged by the group, and "The Flip Side," written by Robin, Laura, and Lisa Brandenburg—Tom was added on drums, along with Dennis McBride on dobro, Doc Browning on harmonica, and Larry Spencer on flügelhorn.

During the rehearsal sessions leading up to the recording session, the Chicks asked Van Schaik to play along with them on some of their other songs, the ones they performed every night. Tom didn't know it at the time, but he was being auditioned for a full-time position with the group.

He also had no idea that it was his friend, Robin, who was putting up the opposition to using drums. It wasn't that she didn't have a high opinion of Tom and his musical abilities, but she felt drums were a sell-out to the bluegrass tradition. Whoever heard of a successful bluegrass band with drums?

The Christmas single, titled "Home on the Radar Range," was manu-factured and distributed by Crystal Clear Sound. It was packaged in a slick, retro designed sleeve that featured the four women dressed in 1950s-style dresses in a mockup kitchen. In the color photograph was Robin, wearing a plaid apron, proudly displaying the baked turkey she just removed from the oven; Laura, wearing a corsage as big as a foot-ball, holding a cup of coffee (or tea) in her gloved hand; Martie holding up wrapped Christmas packages; and Emily, her hands raised in mock admiration of the turkey, sitting on a stool next to a dog wearing a pink bow on its collar.

In their newsletter, which was sent to everyone on the group's mail-ing list, the Chicks invited their fans to hear the Christmas songs per-formed live at the Sons of Hermann Hall in Dallas, where they planned to share the stage with their "musical heroes and friends" Trout Fishing in America, an Arkansas-based bluegrass band.

"You can swing into the Christmas spirit at what is sure to be the so-cial event of the season for a measly five buck-a-roos," said the newslet-ter. "If you bring a homemade cake (it must be from your own radar range), we'll waive the five dollar admission."

The Chicks went on to advise their fans to eat a square meal before coming to their musical cakewalk. "We won't be serving the four basic food groups, pal." The tone of the newsletters was always witty and clever, written in the language of the South.

By the time the Christmas single was released, the Chicks decided they needed to record another self-financed CD. The six-song demo they recorded had fallen on deaf ears in Nashville. If they were going to spend their hard-earned money on recording sessions, they reasoned, they would record CDs they could sell to their fans and not demos that would only be tossed into the trash cans of plush Nashville record labels.

In the year-end newsletter, the Chicks wished happy birthdays to Roy Rogers and Dale Evans, both of whom turned seventy-nine that month.

3

THE MYSTERY OF THE BROKEN PINKIE PROMISE

1992

By early 1992, it was apparent to everyone familiar with the band that the Dixie Chicks possessed a momentum all its own. No one was certain exactly where the group was headed, only that it was driven by women who were hell-bent on going somewhere.

While there were literally hundreds of rival bands across the country, in less than two years, the Dixie Chicks had become a Texas institution, making it one of the most famous "unknown" bands in America.

Thanks to Laura's unrelenting pavement pounding and door knocking, they had signed recently with a Nashville booking agency, Buddy Lee Attractions, becoming one of the few acts without a major recording contract ever represented by that agency. Other recording artists represented by the agency included Ronnie Milsap and Lorrie Morgan.

Although the Chicks were not a big deal in Nashville, they were popular in Texas, one of the best states in the nation in which to book country music acts. The group might not bring in top-dollar headline bookings, but they would make up for that by performing in hundreds of smaller venues.

At the suggestion of Paul Lohr, their contact person at Buddy Lee Attractions, Laura called Nashville manager David Skepner, a respected Nashville music insider who had once managed Loretta Lynn and now represented Riders in the Sky, a popular Nashville-based band that combined ample doses of humor with their music. Skepner agreed to manage the Chicks, perhaps because they had been signed by a booking agency he knew was aggressive on behalf of its clients.

Skepner's first priority was to negotiate a deal for the Chicks with a major label. They had the looks, the talent, the energy, the marketing savvy, and the determination to make it big. All they needed, he reasoned, was a little nudge in the right direction. He quickly learned that selling the Chicks would not be easy. "Number one, we had a tough time just getting the heads of major labels to go see them," he reports. "One day I had the head of a major label tell me, 'Gee, I'm the head of a label, I don't have time to go running around the country listening to acts.'" Recounting that golden moment, Skepner breaks into subdued laughter. "I thought, 'Gee, what business are we in guys?'"

In January 1992 the women returned to Sumet Bernet Studio in Dallas to record another album. As they had done with the previous album, they came prepared to pay cash. "We always waited until we had the money in the bank," Laura explains. "We never did anything in the red, ever. We didn't want the burden of loans. When we bought our equipment, we paid for it the day we took it home. It seemed like the right thing to do. If we needed business cards, we played a show and then we had them [made].

"We went from playing on the street to being booked at everyone's pig roast, literally twenty-five out of thirty days we were playing somewhere—at a bar mitzvah, in someone's backyard, at a club."

For months they had planned to title their next album *Little Ol' Cowgirl,* after a John Ims song they felt represented the spirit of the group. Some of the other songs, especially the self-penned ones, were chosen by trial and error at their live performances.

"We'd pass out little papers that had the songs we were going to play that day, and we'd ask people to rate the songs, first to last," says Laura. "People told us what they wanted to hear."

Whether it was insecurity about the longevity of the group (that is, a belief that they had better accept bookings while they were being offered) or a simple reluctance to say no to cash money, it took the women a while to figure out that if they raised their fee they would perform less but maintain the same income. More important, that would give them time to do more recording.

"We were cheap," laughs Laura. "Give us three hundred and fifty dollars and we would show up all day. Give us a sandwich and we'd play until midnight. We were a big bargain. That's why we worked so much. Then it dawned on us that if maybe we were a little more expensive, we might have more time to do other things."

Little Ol' Cowgirl was a radical departure for the Chicks. For starters, they asked Tom Van Schaik to play on the entire album. Robin was not happy about the addition of a drummer, but, realizing that she was out-numbered three to one, she went along with it, at least for the time being.

The next thing the Chicks did was to hire Grammy-winning pro-ducer Larry Seyer (who had done such a good job on their Christmas single) to engineer and supervise production of the album. He had recorded more than two hundred albums since the early 1970s and by 1992 had become a legendary figure in his own right.

Seyer was to Texas what Billy Sherrill was to Nashville and Chips Mo-man was to Memphis, which is to say a take-charge, behind-the-scenes producer who has a gut instinct about making records.

Enthusiastic about working with the Chicks, Seyer left his home in Austin and went to Dallas, where he checked into a hotel and prepared to spend the two months it would require to record the album the way he wanted it done.

The first order of business was to select the songs. In addition to the songs the Chicks brought to the session, Seyer gathered a box of tapes submitted by songwriters, some of whom he had worked with in the past.

"We went through the [box] and listened to them and voted yes or no and used a point system," he recounts. One of the songs that made the cut, "A Heart That Can," was composed by Seyer's friend, Patty Dickson.

The final list they came up with included four original songs com-posed by the band members, two classic rhythm and blues tunes, and an assortment of western swing and modern country songs, one of which, "A Road Is Just a Road," was composed by Mary Chapin Car-penter and John Jennings.

Once Seyer and the Chicks had selected the songs, Seyer looked for ways to broaden the musical content of the album. "I suggested they needed a steel guitar player for a couple of songs—a friend of mine, Lloyd Maines," recalls Seyer. "I suggested we hire him to come in and play steel guitar."

Maines, who was probably in his early forties at that point, was a musical heavyweight. Behind his back, people often called him the "Godfather" of Texas music (at six-foot-three-inches and two hundred and forty pounds, you didn't call him anything to his face that could be misconstrued). As a member of the Maines Brothers Band, along with siblings Kenny, Donnie, and Steve, he released eight country music albums between 1978 and 1991.

With the disbanding of that group, Maines found more work than he could handle as a session player and as a producer. Among the artists he played for in the studio were Willie Nelson, Hank Williams, Lefty Frizzell, Ray Price, and, yes, even the King himself, Elvis Presley.

"I think I've got a reputation of hanging with it through every thread, every facet of a project," he told the *Austin Chronicle*. "I try not to leave the studio while anything is being laid down, through the whole enchilada. I think bands like that, as opposed to someone that is always going to a phone call or has some other agenda going on. As far as any kind of magical thing, I just try to make the artist feel comfortable and get the absolute best performance out of everybody I work with. To do that, there's a little psychology involved—you have to make them feel good about what they're doing."

As Lloyd Maines was laying down tracks with the Dixie Chicks, his eighteen-year-old daughter, Natalie, was a freshman at West Texas A&M University, which had an enrollment of about five thousand students, in Canyon, Texas (about twenty miles south of Amarillo). She did not declare a major, but from the courses she took it was clear she was considering a career in radio, though exactly what she had in mind is not known, probably not even to Natalie herself.

A diminutive young woman (her height is sometimes given as five-foot-four, but that seems an embellishment), she had battled a weight problem throughout her teen years. Naturally outgoing, she made the cheerleader squad on the strength of her personality. Growing up, she was never grossly overweight, but it was a real struggle for her to limit her weight to what is commonly called "pleasantly plump."

That might have been one reason she initially considered a career in radio. She didn't think she had a television persona and radio allowed her a comfortable margin of anonymity for pursuing her lifelong desire to be a star in some field. Years later, Natalie's second grade teacher at Matt Williams Elementary School in Lubbock, Texas, reminded her of that desire when she telephoned a radio station to talk to Natalie live on the air.

"I've got to tell this story on you," the teacher said. "I was going around the class and asking each of the children a question for them to answer out loud. When I got to you, Natalie, I asked you, 'What is five times three?' You stood up and said, 'Teacher, I don't have to know this stuff—I'm going to be a star.'"

One of the courses Natalie took at West Texas A&M, "Radio Practicum," gave students on-the-job training at the campus's 100-watt radio station, KWTS-FM. RuNell Coons, Natalie's instructor in the course, did not recall her former student when asked, but a quick check of her records revealed that Natalie made an "A" in the subject.

An instructor at West Texas A&M who did remember Natalie was Leigh Browning, director of broadcasting at the school and faculty advisor to the campus radio station. Like all the other students enrolled in the course, Browning explains, Natalie maintained a weekly air shift in which she introduced records and engaged in the impromptu radio chitchat for which announcers are expected to cultivate a talent. The format of the station was college rock, not country, which was in keeping with Natalie's music preferences at that time.

Some people consider Sumet Bernet Studio one of the best in Dallas. With an expansive, forty-foot ceiling, the studio measures sixty-five by fifty feet, large enough to seat an entire orchestra. If the women were intimidated by the size of the studio, they showed no indication of it.

"I put them in a little circle so they could all see each other," producer Larry Seyer recalls. "I put the microphones so they could record looking at each other, but the room was so great I could get near perfect isolation, from one instrument to the other. For example, if Martie was playing her fiddle and Emily was sitting next to her playing a guitar, one instrument would not bleed into the other."

Not gathered in the circle with the girls was drummer Tom Van Schaik, who was isolated from the others in the studio simply because it is difficult to prevent "bleed over" of percussion instruments and most producers prefer to stash drummers in separate, glassed-in enclosures where they can be seen but not heard. Laughs Van Schaik, "I was always outnumbered in that band."

The lighting in the room was "very bright—happy, colorful, and just very clean," says Seyer. "I said then that what the Dixie Chicks need to be is good, wholesome, American fun, because back then there was not much of that. They needed to be squeaky clean and happy and as apple pie as possible, and the studio environment reflected that."

Seyer recorded the entire album on two-inch analog, but brought in so much additional electronic gear that he barely used the studio-equipped console. Says Seyer: "I know the Chicks spent nearly every penny they had to make that record, and even today it sounds phenomenal."

From outward appearances, the Dixie Chicks had everything in place—the right studio, the right producer, a great selection of songs, and what most of the band members felt was needed most, a drummer who had a real feel for the music they wanted to make. However, the Chicks were coming unraveled while they were in the studio.

Robin considered herself the leader of the band. She was more experienced, better "educated" on the nuances of bluegrass music, and, as a school teacher, she felt she had the leadership qualities that were needed to keep an unruly all-girl band in check. Unfortunately, Robin was the only one who felt that way.

As the person who dealt most directly with the public, because she had taken on the added responsibilities of public relations and marketing, Laura was hearing requests for a bolder, more inclusive sound from the Chicks. "That stuff you're doing, it's great," the line went, "but what else can you do?"

Added to that was the fact that the sisters, Martie and Emily, were feeling a need to express themselves more. They were more than a decade younger than either Robin or Laura, and they were beginning to sense a generation gap. It was more pronounced with the schoolmarmish Robin than with Laura, even though they were the same age. For some reason, the sisters felt more of a kinship with Laura, whose spontaneous personality made her seem younger and more adventurous.

The first three-to-one vote had come over the addition of a drummer. "Up until that point, they had never played with a drummer—they had always set their own time," Van Schaik says. "It was a struggle for them at first to get them to relinquish that to me and to listen to me. A couple of times Larry stopped the tape and said, 'Listen to the drummer.' But they settled into it."

Robin accepted her defeat with good grace.

The second three-to-one vote at the session came over who would sing lead vocals. The sisters agreed with Laura that she should sing lead on half of the songs on the new album, although they did not know at that point exactly how many songs would be on the album.

"With any band that has two lead vocalists, you're going to have those two personalities wanting to be out front, wanting to be the center—and they had to divide the time out equally," says Van Schaik. "At that point, I think Robin decided that was not the direction she wanted to go."

Again, Robin seemingly took her defeat on the chin, although there were times during the session when emotions ran high.

When it came to how the songs would be recorded, a fifth vote was counted—that of producer Larry Seyer. "Larry guided the whole thing, from what I can recall," Van Schaik remarks. "If there was a difference of opinion, he'd say, 'I'm the producer and this is the decision I am making.' Some things between Laura and Robin and Robin and the other girls didn't go well. Robin was a very strict bluegrasser. She was the last one to give in to having drums. She was the last one to give in to plugging in her guitar. Robin was fighting sort of an inner battle. Listening to the album, you can hear a difference in the songs she sings and the ones Laura sings. The ones Robin sings are more traditional, much more low key with the percussion."

One of the songs the women struggled with was "Aunt Mattie's Quilt," written by Robin and her friend Lisa Brandenburg. The song was recorded with drums, but when the time came to add the vocals, according to Van Schaik, Robin staged a mini-revolt.

"Robin put her foot down," he says. "She said she didn't like the drums, that was just too modern. I had to retract my work after it had been done. Looking back, I think that song was when Robin realized she was either going to have to move on or give in."

Seyer was aware of the discord among the women, who, fortunately, all lived in separate residences and did not have to face each other outside the studio. However, he didn't need to think too much about the differences of opinion because any disagreements were settled by a collective vote. "There were some lively debates over what songs would be chosen, but nothing outstanding," he says. "You want to do that for all albums."

Van Schaik recalls the sisters trying to remain as neutral as possible during the band's decision-making. "Most of the tension was between Laura and Robin, and that gets down to the fact that the lead singer wants the focus," he says. "The sisters would hang in the background and hear both sides and then render their decision. For as young as they were, they were pretty amazing. Every one of them was a great player.

The sisters were far above the other two, as far as their playing is concerned, but I always enjoyed Robin's songwriting and, to this day, I still love Laura's voice. She has this pure voice that is really pretty."

What impressed Seyer about the session, he says in retrospect, was the musicianship of the sisters. "You could sing or play them something and they would hear it immediately," he says. "They are both naturals. Emily, especially. She was playing banjo back then, and banjo is kind of a hard thing to sell for country music, so I suggested she try guitar. She wasn't used to playing a guitar, so she restrung it like a banjo and played banjo parts on an acoustic guitar. We did that on a couple of tunes."

Of the four of them, Seyer had the highest opinion, musically, of Emily. Not only could she play multiple instruments (dobro, guitar, bass, and banjo), she could fingerpick her way through a song with the best of them. "Some people are like old souls in young bodies," Seyer says. "Emily's an old soul. Even at that age, she knew things that people twenty years older knew. In some ways she was older than Martie. That really stood out about Emily."

Seyer liked the way Martie quickly caught on to musical licks and phrases that he suggested she try. "I would hum a melody line—Martie, try this—and she would play it right away. Usually, it takes a pretty seasoned player to do that, but Martie could do it with no problem."

Seyer liked Laura's business sense and how she was always "on," a characterization that arises time and time again among others when the singer's name is mentioned. "She is like a light bulb that never goes out," he says. "Always a happy face."

Seyer's assessment of Robin is more restrained: "Very determined, methodical . . . it's x-y-z, then it's a-b-c."

Once they had put down the basic tracks for the album, they flew Lloyd Maines in from Lubbock to play steel guitar on several of the songs. Maines listened to the songs, then played his parts, all without much fanfare.

"They were very much impressed with Lloyd," Seyer says. "I honestly didn't know he had a daughter at that time. Natalie would have still been in high school or just starting college. Lloyd and Laura became good friends, and Laura ended up hiring Lloyd to do several shows with them."

Recording *Little Ol' Cowgirl,* says Seyer, was unlike any other project he had ever worked on. "The girls would look so good," he says. "You're producing this record. You've got these gorgeous women in front of you and they look fabulous and they're playing their butts off. I think it was one of the best times of my life."

Between takes, the women let their hair down, literally, and took turns using a mini-trampoline Martie brought from her home. Soon they were engaging in group calisthenics led by Martie.

While Laura tried to organize a sewing bee and Robin educated the ladies on world events, shy Emily slipped out the back door and hung out with a rap band that was recording in an adjacent studio. Laura joked about Emily's excursion into urban music by saying she felt it was done to get help with her new song, "Yo! Dale!"

Work on *Little Ol' Cowgirl* was completed by March 1992, but the release date was delayed for weeks, while the Chicks' manager shopped the tape in Nashville. It can take months to produce an album, but, with only a half dozen or so record labels in Nashville interested in listening to tapes, the suspense often is over within a matter of days. While it is not unusual for publishers to spend weeks, even months, considering a book proposal, record label artists and repertoire executives will usually give a thumbs up or down the same day they listen. The problem lies in getting them to listen.

Little Ol' Cowgirl was an outstanding album, and the Chicks knew it. The vocals, the instrumentation, the production quality—all were at or beyond Nashville's highest standards. As had happened with the previous album, there were no takers for *Little Ol' Cowgirl,* not even with the support of a respected manager.

Adding to the woes of the Dixie Chicks was the fact that they were just so attractive. Any male record executive who signed the group would most likely be accused of doing it for sexual reasons. As good as they were, the Dixie Chicks just seemed to be more trouble than they were worth. (In the late 1980s, the head of a major record label in Nashville revealed that he would not allow a woman to come into his office alone, so fearful was he of what people would say—or, even worse, what legal actions could result if there were allegations of sexual wrongdoing.)

Rebuffed again, the women prepared to release the album themselves, a possibility they had prepared for from the beginning. Behind the scenes, Robin was still smarting over the changes the group was undergoing. She was not a happy Chick.

To make matters worse, Laura, Martie, and Emily talked of adding drummer Tom Van Schaik to the group's touring band. To Robin, this sparked a crisis of a different magnitude. The addition of a drummer to a single session was one thing, for it signified nothing more substantial than an artistic flirtation. Taking a drummer with them on the road was something else entirely.

By spring, the release of *Little Ol' Cowgirl* seemed stalled. They knew the new material was the best they had done to date. They knew their fans would expect them to perform it the way it sounded on the record. How could they possibly do justice to fourteen new songs on their playlist, all of which bore the unmistakable rhythms of a drummer and percussionist? To Laura, Emily, and Martie, the answer was simple.

In yet another three-to-one vote the Dixie Chicks hired Tom Van Schaik as their full-time drummer. They announced it in their newsletter, which they published whenever convenient. "We're now a one-MAN band with the initiation of the Drummin' Dutchman, Tom Van Schaik, into chickdom," said the newsletter. "He's a great percussionist and has a dadgum degree to prove it!" The newsletter apologized for the delay in the release of the new album, adding that the recording session had left the group "impoverished and ever more codependent."

Even after the girls started traveling in their van with Van Schaik, feelings about his presence remained an issue. It did not appear to be serious—there were no cat fights or anything like that—but there was lots of passive-aggressive hostility that was expressed verbally.

They would be in the van and the topic of food would arise. Martie, a vegetarian, would not eat in a Mexican restaurant or a steak house no matter what. Laura, Emily, and Van Schaik preferred Mexican and steak, so that left Robin as the supreme arbitrator as they drove the van in circles looking for a place that would satisfy all of their dietary requirements.

"Meanwhile, we'd be passing all sorts of Luby's Cafeteria, Tortilla Factories, Pie House, perfectly great places to eat, but Robin transformed herself into a banshee and declared that since we all hired a drummer we should be eating at the such and such truck stop," laughs Laura, a reference to Robin's insistence that they were paying the drummer so much they couldn't afford anything better than a truck stop.

"End of discussion. But it was a small but unending price to pay for per-cussion."

In March 1992, before the album was even mixed, *Dallas Life* maga-zine stated the obvious: that the Chicks' hopes were riding high on the album. "So much depends on this record," reported the publication. It quoted Martie as saying: "I hope our fans won't be disappointed. It's got drums on every track. It's no longer bluegrass, but we have to make a living, and you can't do that playing bluegrass."

Ed Bernet, owner of Sumet Bernet Studio, told *Dallas Life* he felt good about the band's future. Said Bernet: "They make people happy, they're so pretty and so good. Pretty from a man's point of view isn't a nega-tive. If they weren't pretty they'd still be good, but being young, pretty, and talented is an unbeatable combination."

With the release of the new album scheduled for May at the earliest, the Chicks carried on with a busy touring schedule. They were booked solid in March, with appearances at the Lone Star Roadhouse in New York City, the Iron Horse in Northampton, Massachusetts, and the Birchmere in Alexandria, Virginia. They drove their van to each venue.

Laura, Martie, and Emily were excited about the new album, excited about having Tom in the band, and excited about the future in general.

By contrast, Robin was discouraged and pessimistic about the future. To her way of thinking, the Dixie Chicks were out of control, well on their way to becoming another hit-seeking country act. Robin was right, of course.

Laura was ambitious. She wanted the trappings that went with fame and fortune.

Emily and Martie had youth tugging at their apron strings. They were on fire with the power of their music and they wanted to be turned loose to find its level. Women that age tend to be pumped full of new-found, surging hormones to begin with. Add to that the spiritual elec-tricity that comes with blossoming artistic talent, and you get a mixture that is hard to rein in.

One day while they were on the road, they stopped at a Denny's restaurant for lunch. "Tensions were at a high level," recalls Laura. "Martie and Emily and me, we loved our new drummer, but Robin didn't feel the same way. We respected that, but we still had to go with major-ity rule. It was one against drums and three in favor of drums."

To Laura's way of thinking, women quite naturally do business a little differently than men. "There are a lot of things that girl partnerships do that are different," she explains. "I think we bank differently. I know we balance our checkbooks different. It's a good different."

While having lunch at Denny's that day, they professed their loyalty to one another and their desire to make the ongoing relationship work. What they needed, someone said, was a gesture, a symbolic joining of spirit.

"We made a Pinkie Promise that day in Denny's," Laura says. "That's when you link pinkies and you say, 'Well, OK, forevermore we're not going to discuss it, and we're not going to look back.'"

Laura believed in the power of the pinkie pull. Years later, while telling the story, there was a sadness in her voice. Said Laura, "Most people hung onto the pinkie pull idea—others didn't."

When they returned to Texas in April or May, it was with a belief that everything would work out. They had been through too much together for it not to work out. On stage, they were expanding beyond the addition of a drummer.

Lloyd Maines, whose tasty steel guitar licks had added so much to *Little Ol' Cowgirl,* was often hired for live shows, especially when the Chicks opened for male country stars such as Jerry Jeff Walker and others. About Maines' contribution to the group, Laura said in a 1999 interview: "I thought he really elevated our music with his playing. This is a guy with music in his bones. It was a great relationship, a musical bonus to all of us."

Despite all the stress and uncertainty of the delayed album—and the continuing discord among the women over what direction the band should take—they had to keep going. Performing was what put food on the table and allowed Laura to buy clothing and school supplies for her eleven-year-old daughter, Asia Abraham.

The Dixie Chicks stayed busy throughout 1992. They made their debut on the Grand Ole Opry and performed on *Nashville Now,* the hour-long Nashville Network cable TV show hosted by Ralph Emery. (In their newsletter they bragged that they had actually seen the legendary host without makeup.)

No booking was too small or too far away to accept. The women even found time to perform at the Southwestern High School auditorium in Hanover, Pennsylvania, for Martie and Emily's grandfather's eightieth birthday party.

Almost as lucrative as their performance fees was the money they were making on merchandise sales. Dixie Chicks T-shirts sold for fifteen dollars for the short sleeve designs and twenty dollars for the long sleeve shirts. They even had shirts for children that bore the message "I'm A Dixie Chicklet."

In over thirty years of writing about music, the author has never seen an unsigned band more skilled at using merchandise to market itself. Had the technology existed then for them to market themselves over the Internet, the possibilities would have been endless.

"I still have pals in Nashville in A&R and promotion, and they say, 'How in the world did you get this band national without a public relations machine behind you?'" Laura related in 1999. "It was hard. It took enormous effort. We'd send out postcards and letters telling our schedule. We told about everything we played, even if it was private. We just wanted everything in there. 'Lookie, you can hire us! Nothing is too small or stupid for us to play.' That persona carried us a long way. . . . I bet I wrote a million handwritten letters. The way you get asked back is you stay in touch. You keep them thinking about you. . . ."

ROBIN TWITTERS, FLIES THE COOP

1992

With no interest in *Little Ol' Cowgirl* from the major labels in Nashville, the Dixie Chicks decided to release it themselves. Two of the benefits of a band recording and releasing its own CD are that the finished product will sound and look like what the artists envisioned. In the case of *Little Ol' Cowgirl,* the finished CD sounded like a million bucks, and the packaging was as slick as anything produced in Nashville.

The cover photo on the insert shows a little girl, dressed in red cowgirl boots, skirt, and hat, with one hand resting on a wagon wheel and the other propped sassily on her hip. Inside, there is a group photo of the band, with the four women standing around Laura's surreal green bass designed to look like a giant cactus. Interestingly, Robin, who is seen standing next to Laura, has her back turned somewhat to the others. Other individual photos were in color and captured the women with their instruments.

As far as packaging went, it put to shame many of the products being issued by the major labels. The color photography was bright and straightforward; it featured both the group and the individual members. The lyrics of the songs were printed in full, and the contributions each band member made to the album were explained. It was a tight package.

Internally, the Dixie Chicks were going through hell, but you couldn't tell it by looking at them. To publicize the release of *Little Ol' Cowgirl* they rented the Majestic Ballroom, one of Dallas's most opulent entertainment venues. It was an old movie theater that still had its original seats in place, along with an intimate balcony that overlooked the expansive stage. The public was invited to attend the party.

"I was impressed that four little girls from Texas would rent a huge ballroom like that and have thousands of people here," producer Larry Seyer declares. "Trout Fishing in America, the group from Arkansas, was there with them, and someone else played, too. Of course, the Dixie Chicks played, and they were great."

Music store owner Jay Rury said it was the largest venue in which he had ever seen the Chicks perform. Says Rury: "They put on one hell of a show. The little gal on the cover [who had been selected by the photographer] was there and came out and danced to the title number. Afterward they stood in the anteroom and signed autographs for everyone who wanted them until everyone was gone.

"The thing about the Chicks in the early days was that they were so honest. They weren't standoffish at all. You felt like family when you went to their concerts, and when they sang to you, it was fresh and open."

Dallas embraced the new album. Airplay was immediate, and within days one of the cuts that featured Laura on lead, "A Heart That Can," was getting airplay across the country.

"The Dixie Chicks were retro before retro was cool," says drummer Van Schaik. "Early on, when they were doing more of the cowgirl stuff, Nashville did not have a clue about what to do with them. At that time, all the hat acts were really popular in Nashville. They looked at the Chicks and said, 'That's not what we're doing now.' I kept scratching my head because they were selling so many CDs. It was like Nashville was saying, 'Well, what do we do with them?'"

One day, quite by accident, they encountered an Atlantic Records executive at one of their concerts. His name was Al Cooley. "He came up to me, and he said he was with Atlantic Records, and I said, 'Yeah, and we're gonna have tacos at midnight,' and I walked off, and he said, 'No, really, here's my card,'" Laura recalls. "He turned out to be very nice. He told us some things that were hard to hear, about reinventing ourselves, about taking each album in a new direction . . . I don't know why we had our hands over our ears, but we didn't take heed, and I think he genuinely wanted to nurture our artistic direction."

When asked about the encounter in 1999, Cooley confirmed Laura's recollection of the meeting. He had only been on the job (as head of artists and repertoire) for two weeks when he went to Austin as a guest of Robert Earl Keen, a popular Texas recording artist who knew just about everyone in the business.

"One night we went to a Dixie Chicks show," recalls Cooley, adding that he was dressed in a scroungy T-shirt and looked like anything but a record executive. "I'm pretty sure we both looked pretty funky."

When the Chicks asked Cooley what he thought about the band, he was direct: "I think Laura should be the lead singer, and I think you should add some drums." (At that point Van Schaik was still not on the payroll full-time.)

"Atlantic came very close to signing the group," Cooley confides. "Rick Blackburn [the head of the label] almost did a deal with them because of the single, 'You Send Me.' Rick kept saying, 'I think radio would play this song.'"

"You Send Me" is the soulful Sam Cooke rhythm and blues song on which Laura sang lead. The harmonies on the song were exquisite, and Lloyd Maines bridged the gap between R&B and country with a series of delicate slide maneuvers that kept the music honest. Added to that mix was Emily's fine banjo work on a fast-paced exit from the song. With Atlantic Records' long history of rhythm and blues, it would have been a good release for its Nashville office.

After sharing his observations with the women—and watching Robin walk away in a huff—he and Keen helped them load their equipment into their van. It was the least they could do.

In early summer 1992, not long after the release of *Little Ol' Cowgirl,* Robin dropped a bombshell: She was leaving the group. An upcoming performance in Austin would be her last, she told her bandmates. After that, they wouldn't have Robin around to outvote on every group issue.

"Robin did go on stage [in Austin]," recalls Laura. "She didn't sing very loud or play very hard, but she did participate and get us through the night. We didn't see her again for a long, long time."

Laura, Martie, and Emily were stunned by Robin's departure. They were like a lot of married couples in which one of the partners keeps saying, "Now if you do that one more time, I'm out of here," and the other partner keeps thinking they have received a reprieve until the next crisis, when in fact they have run out of reprieves. Even if you know in your heart that your significant other is leaving you, the actual act itself is always painful. So it was with Robin's departure.

On August 5, 1992, Robin entered into an agreement with the Dixie Chicks, according to court records, whereby the two-year partnership would be dissolved and then reconstituted under the same name under the ownership of Laura, Martie, and Emily.

In return for bowing out of the group, Robin asked for $14,500 in cash, the right to identify herself as a former Dixie Chick, statutory license royalties for the three Dixie Chicks recordings on which she had participated as a cowriter—*Thank Heavens for Dale Evans, Little Ol' Cowgirl*, and *Home on the Radar Range*—and twenty-five percent of any future revenues generated by those recordings.

The agreement also contained several unusual conditions that are indicative of the hard feelings between Robin and the others, including an agreement that each of the partners would refrain from making "slanderous" remarks about each other and an agreement that any media releases that mentioned Robin Macy by name would be submitted for her advance approval.

On September 15, 1992, all four women signed the agreement.

"Martie, Emily, and I were hardly apart in those first few weeks [after the split]," Laura recalls. "We didn't know if we were going to fold or not. We had contracts that we had signed. We had received deposits. We couldn't say, 'I'm sorry. We imploded. Goodbye!'"

Robin's departure raised real questions about the group's professional survival. Robin had carried half the weight of the lead vocals, and her harmonies were an important ingredient in the Chicks sound. Emily could play guitar, but her mainstays were banjo and dobro. If they hired a guitarist, Laura could step in and do all the lead vocals and the sisters could provide any harmony that was needed.

The one thing the women knew they did not want to do was to recruit another Chick. Once they conceptualized their next step, they wasted no time taking it. "We hired an incredible guitarist named Matthew Benjamin," says Laura. "He really came in and saved the day. He knew our music and what he didn't know he learned in an hour. We never missed a gig."

The timing of Robin's departure was awkward for the band. They were faced with promoting a CD that had a photograph of four women on

the cover. The first thing they had to do was shoot new publicity photos that showed just the three of them.

Reaction to the shakeup was predictable. Those who wanted the
Dixie Chicks to remain a hard-core bluegrass band were unhappy to see
Robin depart. Those who preferred the band to branch out into new di-
rections saw her departure as an indication that the Chicks had ambitions beyond the bluegrass circuit.

Music store owner Jay Rury was among those sorry to see the change,
although he is quick to add that he remained Dallas's number one
Chicks fan. "Robin was more into the style that I liked personally," Rury
told the author. "I liked her voice, her style, her type of music. When
she left the Dixie Chicks, that voice and that harmony just dropped off.
At the time I didn't like it [her departure]. I wish she hadn't, but she had
her reasons."

Laura, Martie, and Emily knew it was pretty much out of their hands.
They went back out on stage as if nothing had ever happened. If anything, they offered their fans more of themselves than ever before.
More music, more talk, more onstage energy—that quality women
have, that genetic link, that allows them to nurture the feelings of others when what they really want to do is crawl under a rock and die. The
Chicks were an all-girl band, not an imitation male group, and they
played the gender card for all it was worth.

Fortunately, the Dixie Chicks had several bookings out of the Dallas
area before the time came for them to face their hard-core Dallas–Fort
Worth fans at the Caravan of Dreams festival in late August 1992. They
need not have worried. "Chicks still click," read the headline of the *Fort
Worth Star-Telegram*. "Yes—the Dallas-based cowgirl band that's ruled
the roost for the past three years will indeed survive as a trio," read the
review, written by Shirley Jinkins.

Robin would be missed for her stage persona and her harmonies,
concluded the critic, but Laura was more than up to the challenge of
handling the lead vocals. "Instrumentally, there's not much difference.
Emily has taken over a lot more of the bass from Laura and given up a
few banjo solos, but that's about it. The rest is as tight and tuneful as
ever, paced by Martie's magnificent fiddle."

By the end of the program, which was marked by a standing ovation,
the Chicks clearly had "re-bonded" with their fans. It was exactly the
reaffirmation of faith the Chicks needed.

During one of the touching moments of the Caravan of Dreams performance, Martie stepped up to the microphone to make an announcement (something she was loathe to do). Vince Gill had offered her a job as the fiddle player in his band, she told the crowd, which suddenly grew very quiet and restless at hearing that bit of news. Then in a moment of unbridled sisterhood, she gazed across the stage at Laura and Emily, and she smiled—a smile so embracing that it has to be seen to be believed—and she said she had turned down the offer, adding, "I could never leave you guys."

The *Fort Worth Star-Telegram* reviewer concluded regarding their performance, "Whatever ground they've lost with established fandom should be regained without much trouble, and after all, there's a whole world of new people out there, too."

Less than a week later, the Dixie Chicks traveled to Santa Monica, California, where they performed at At My Place, a club that had a reputation as being friendly to up-and-coming artists. "What a great place to play," commented Laura as she stepped up to the microphone. "No chicken wire!"

In the audience that night was *Cashbox* writer Robert Adels, who wrote a glowing review of the performance in the trade publication. "Dixie Chicks deserve to be country's next Cinderella story thanks to the power and charm of their just-released second album, *Little Ol' Cowgirl* and the magic they make in concert . . . ," he wrote.

Adels particularly liked "Pink Toenails," a song from the new album written by Laura and Martie. The song begins with an unexpected trumpet solo that leads into a bluesy, country-swing number that seems to capture the attitude and sass of the new Chicks. It was exactly the type of material, Adels concluded, that would allow the Chicks to add alternative rock fans to their existing country base.

"Dixie Chicks should do for women on country indie labels what Garth and Billy Ray [Cyrus] have done for men on country majors," he said. "They've got the looks to win America's hearts—and the talent to keep the love affair growing for years."

The Dixie Chicks could hardly believe their own ears. They had taken the biggest gamble of their short professional lives, and it was paying off. Sales for *Little Ol' Cowgirl* were soaring both in stores and out on the road. Manufactured and distributed by Crystal Clear Sound of Dallas, the album achieved sales of forty-eight thousand, according to

Laura, compared to sales of the first album of less than twenty thousand. It was an impressive performance by an indie release, coming at a time when most country releases on the majors failed to reach those numbers.

"They were developing an interest down through Texas and everywhere they played," says David Skepner, their manager at the time. "It's amazing how many CDs they could sell from the back of their [van]. They were on the road making a good living, whether they had a major deal or not, which is what acts are starting to do now. Why should I go with a major record company when I'm never going to see anything [financially]. In some ways, the Dixie Chicks were ahead of their time."

Encouraged by that first rush of success following the breakup, the Dixie Chicks loaded up their van, complete with their new male guitarist and drummer, and Humphrey, and went on the road. Before Robin left they had customized the van, adding bunk beds and a curtain of protective netting to catch airborne Chicks whenever the brakes were applied a little too suddenly (not an infrequent occurrence).

In their newsletter, the Chicks said the van looked like an animal control vehicle. "We're selecting curtain fabric and a potpourri scent," they said. "By the way, does anyone know anything about attaching seatbelts to bean bag chairs?"

In addition to their musical instruments, the newsletter went on to report, amplifiers, equalizers, microphones, and Tom's drum kit, the girls found they needed a few items not found on Garth's tour bus—four sets of hot rollers, a family size container of Aquanet, sixteen pairs of cowboy boots (well, maybe Garth could match them here), and "six sticky humans with snackpacks 'n trailmix."

Things looked so bright for the Chicks that they started bumping heads with their new Nashville booking agency. "I stepped on [their] toes a few times," admits Laura, who found it difficult to relinquish control of some of the business aspects of the group's activities. "They started booking us after we'd played so many shows for so many people, so we had a real good foothold here in the Southern marketplace. Then they said, 'OK we'll start booking you, but when you get a booking spin-off from that show, that's our booking too.'"

That didn't go over too well with Laura, who didn't want to pay the agency commissions for bookings the girls had been doing repeatedly for years. Lynch stuck to her guns on the recurring old bookings, and the agency agreed to a hands-off attitude toward them. "I probably tried to keep control of too much for too long," she admits. "But when we told people to call the Nashville office, they felt betrayed that they could not talk to us directly, and I hated doing that to people."

The Chicks followed a strict set of rules on the road. The first, according to drummer Tom Van Schaik, who today remembers it with good humor, dealt with their hair and costumes. "Their slogan was 'more is more,'" he says. "The amount of hair, rhinestones—it was not a real big issue, but they spent time getting it [the hair] as big as possible in the beginning."

Another rule dealt with alcohol consumption. "The rule for everyone was that there would be no drinking [during a performance]," Laura says. "When we were on the road, the bar to every honky tonk was open to us, whatever the band wanted to drink. We encouraged the band to wait until the last break of the night.

"We [the women] never did it because we were handling the money and sometimes people paid us in cash, and the merchandising had to be inventoried and we had to have a brain on for that. Plus, it wasn't attractive to us. It just wasn't in the cards for us to be partying on the road across the country, and it wasn't anyone's real desire anyway."

LITTLE OL' COWGIRLS ROPE 'EM HIGH AND RIDE 'EM HARD

1993

Emily breezed onto the van, her eyes as big as saucers. "You'll never believe what happened to me," she said. Everyone else was already on the van, waiting for Emily, the youngest of the Dixie Chicks until Natalie Maines joined the group in 1995, and their attitude was pretty much that it had better be a damned good story to justify the long wait. They were ready to hit the road—and sitting in a parked van waiting for Emily was *way down* on their list of fun things to do.

Emily didn't disappoint.

The incident occurred sometime in 1992 or 1993, no one recalls the exact date, for when you are touring with a band, days, weeks, months, all merge into one big blur.

For the past several months, Emily had been dating a man she met in high school. He wasn't very tall and when he stood at his full height, the top of his head barely brushed against the bottom of her chin. The relationship had about run its course, but Emily had never found breaking up easy to do.

Since she was out on the road so much with the Chicks, avoiding him seemed easier than dumping him. Besides, he had a key to her house and kept her plants watered when she was out of town. Why mess with a good thing?

The problem was Emily had met someone else, the lead singer of a rocking country band that was packing honky-tonks all across Texas. Unlike Emily's boyfriend, he was a tall, heavyset fellow who towered over her. Out of respect for his Texas-sized girth and his steer-roping passion for privacy, let's just call him Big Fellah.

The evening before the band was scheduled to go out on the road, Big Fellah spent the night at Emily's house, Emily later explained to her bandmates, though she hurried past that part of the story.

The next morning, as Emily rushed through a shower, she heard a sound that sent shivers up her spine—shades of *Psycho*. Someone was coming in the back door. In an instant, she knew who the intruder was. She had not called her boyfriend when she returned home the previous day, for obvious reasons. Thinking she was on the road, he had stopped by her house to water her plants. What a guy!

Quickly, she jumped out of the shower and threw on a towel, then dashed into the kitchen just in time to greet him at the door. She was dripping wet.

The boyfriend was obviously surprised to see her.

"You should call before you come over," Emily said, uttering a phrase that sets off alarm bells in any male's built-in security system. The boyfriend looked at Emily, then he looked in the direction of the bedroom, putting two and two together.

Suddenly, his dark eyes flashed, and he bolted for the other room.

"No, no!" Emily cried out, grabbing hold of his belt as he went by.

Like a Spanish conquistador, the boyfriend charged ahead, dragging Emily behind him. She told her bandmates she was moving so fast that she felt like "a water-skier" skimming across the surface of a lake. They liked that image of their waterlogged baby Chick being towed across the kitchen floor, barefoot, her towel waving in the breeze.

When Emily and the boyfriend skied into the bedroom, Big Fellah rose to his feet, the loud voices having alerted him to possible trouble. The boyfriend took one look at Big Fellah and stopped dead in his tracks. He tossed a few choice words Emily's way, then left as quickly as he had entered, leaving the towel-draped Chick speechless.

For nearly four years (1989–1993), the Dixie Chicks cultivated an image of beautiful women having good, clean fun. For the most part, the girls were exactly as advertised. What didn't show on stage was the fact that they all had normal personal lives. They had boyfriends, lovers, romantic intrigues, and close calls galore.

Dixie Chicks drummer Tom Van Schaik says there was never as much romance on the road as you would expect. "They pretty much kept their private lives to themselves," he reports. "The couple of times there were [men around], they were acting as drivers, so it wasn't too bad because I didn't have to drive and that was fine with me . . . generally speaking, boyfriends never got in the way."

The Chicks all had boyfriends, says producer Larry Seyer, "but they hardly ever came into the studio. The girls didn't come into the studio to party. It was too expensive. When we worked, we worked. If boyfriends showed up, it was like, 'Here's your lunch, good-bye.' They didn't stick around." (Most musicians don't like to leave the studio during a session, so it is customary for them to order out or ask friends to bring their meals to the studio.)

In the early- to mid-1990s, Texas State Fair goers would have been hard-pressed to come across a more glamorous, energetic, or sexually-charged group than the Dixie Chicks. The fair is held each October in Dallas, and for years civic leaders have proclaimed it to be the largest in the nation.

With Robin out of the picture, the women really let down their hair and took the state fair audience for a spin, focusing on the music, but not ignoring the perfumed net of sexuality they knew they cast upon their audiences.

After the first of several sets, the Dixie Chicks left the stage, with Laura going to the van and the others leaving to scope out the fairground. Laura was only in the van a few minutes when there came a knock on the door.

"Pardon me," said a young cowboy who was dressed in a starched cowboy shirt, western hat, and boots (let's just call him Hoss). "Do you have a picture I can buy?" He motioned back toward the gate. "They said you sold pictures."

The Chicks made as much from merchandising as they did from performing, so they never lost an opportunity to sell a photo, CD, or T-shirt. By the time Laura returned to the door with the photograph, the visitor had assumed all the physical characteristics of a Brad Pitt-like, Texas rancher. Earnest. Square-jawed. Honest as the day is long.

"Ma'am," said Hoss, politely taking off his hat, "would you mind signing this picture?"

Laura invited him into the van. She sat down and offered him a chair. He seemed ill at ease, yet respectful, so she felt comfortable allowing him in. Besides that, he was everything a cowgirl dreamed of in a cowboy—tall, square-shouldered, bright-eyed, and handsome as all get out.

Still dressed in her stage costume, Laura slipped off her boots.

"These boots are sure hard on a person's feet," she said.

"Want me to massage your feet?" Hoss asked, his voice trembling.

"Why, sure," said Laura.

He massaged first one foot, then the other. Then his hands moved up her calves as he massaged her legs, moving ever so slowly, devoting the serious attention to each calf that he would devote to any job given to him by his ranch foreman. Then his hands moved up onto her thighs, rustling her floral print skirt as he gently massaged her tired, aching muscles. It was the most relaxing photo signing Laura ever had.

"Thank you," she said, not knowing what else to say.

As he was leaving the van, Hoss looked back at Laura and spoke, his words coming from nowhere: "I love you, baby." He said it just like he must have heard it said in the movies.

Laura, slightly dazed by the experience, asked, "Well . . . what's your name?"

Hoss threw open the door to the van, the sunlight kicking against his hat. "I'll see you after the next show," he said, and tipped his Stetson. Then he was gone.

Laura never saw the cowboy again.

On January 20, 1993, the Dixie Chicks performed for President Bill Clinton and Vice President Al Gore at the Tennessee Inaugural Ball at the Washington Hilton, along with Jimmy Buffet and his Coral Reefer Band, Kathy Mattea, Rosanne Cash, Lou Reed, and others. Most of the guests were dressed in formal dinner wear, but the Chicks showed up in their glitzy, retro-cowgirl outfits, all ready to shine.

The Secret Service wouldn't allow them into the ballroom until they were screened by a metal detector. Emily volunteered to go first. The blushing Service Service agent, who looked closer to twenty than thirty, ran the device up, down, and over Emily's body, saving the most sensitive area for last—her breasts.

To Emily's horror, as he moved the hand-held device over her chest, the alarm went off . . . *beep, beep, beep* . . . The Secret Service agent was as surprised as anyone there. At first, he was speechless, his eyes understandably glued to Emily's fringe-covered chest, which by that time had begun to heave somewhat.

For a moment everything in the room stopped, as if someone had touched the pause button on a VCR. The other Chicks froze in their tracks, fighting an urge to run for the door, but thinking, "What on earth does that girl have in her bra?"

The Secret Service agent pointed to the shiny, silver fringe on Emily's costume. "Is that metallic?" he asked.

"Yessssss!" Emily said.

The agent grinned and motioned her into the room.

When the Al Gore family arrived with their children, they took one look at the crew of performers assembled backstage and decided that they wanted Al Gore III and his bodyguards to hang out with the Dixie Chicks. They deposited the lucky youngster in the care of the Chicks, who mothered him throughout the evening.

"Ever striving for a Cowgirl fashion statement, we donned our snappy new duds for the occasion," the Chicks reported in their newsletter. "Various elegant folks were whispering, 'They must be from Dallas.' I think it was the hair which we poofed up bigger'n trash can lids!"

Backstage, Martie chatted with singer Paul Simon, Laura struck up a conversation with Jimmy Buffet (who told her that he was pleased to meet her, but, frankly, had never heard of the Dixie Chicks), and Emily confronted Johnny Cash, face-to-face, when they both reached for the same deviled crab puff. Emily won the puff-off with Cash, but who would want to slap Emily's hand away from anything?

After performing at the Inaugural Ball, the Chicks left town in their van, swinging down by Alexandria, Virginia, for a show at the Birchmere, then heading north until they reached the New Jersey Turnpike.

When time came for a lunch break, they spotted a Roy Rogers Hamburger Restaurant and, true to cowgirl tradition, pulled off the turnpike to dine with other fans of the singing King of Cowboys. As the girls were going into the restaurant—actually it was one of those monster-sized truck stops—they noticed a limousine parked near the entrance. If there's anything that will catch the eye of a Dixie Chick, it is a limousine gathering dust.

Once they were seated at a table and the girls had an opportunity to scan the restaurant, Emily spotted a table of jewelry-bedecked men sitting across the room. The men had limousine written all over them. "I swear, that's Michael Jackson's father!" Emily said, barely able to keep her voice down.

"Right, Emmie!" said Laura. "We're on the road in Pennsylvania, and that's not Michael Jackson's father."

"It is!" she insisted.

The more Emily looked at the man, the more convinced she was that it was Michael Jackson's father. She has an excellent memory for faces and has astonished her traveling companions more than once with unexpected star spottings.

Finally, Emily mustered her courage and approached the table of middle-aged African American men, most of whom probably were a little bit on the paranoid side to be eating in a Roy Rogers restaurant, especially one located in a big-ass truck stop.

"Let me introduce myself," Emily said, extending her hand to the man she just knew was Michael Jackson's father. "I'm Emily Erwin, a member of the Dixie Chicks."

Surprised, the man took her hand (who wouldn't?) and gazed into the eyes of one of the most striking women in American music. What could he possibly do but proclaim the truth? "Nice to meet you," he said. "I'm Joseph Jackson."

"Oh, you're Michael's father!"

"Yes," he said.

Emily cut her eyes back around toward her cohorts, who by that time were clustered together like hens on a roost, and she let them know, by her I-told-you-so glance, that she had struck pay dirt. After exchanging a few pleasantries, Emily ran back to the table and told the Chicks everything that had happened.

Together, they ran out to the van and gathered an armful of Dixie Chicks CDs, T-shirts, and other promotional materials, and then they rushed back inside, where they dumped their memorabilia onto Joseph Jackson's table. Smiling broadly, but looking somewhat perplexed, he posed for photographs with the Chicks and assured them that, yes, certainly he would be sure to listen to their tapes, and then he would tell Michael *all* about them.

Being on the road with the Dixie Chicks may not have been a thrill a minute, but it was pretty close at times, recalls drummer Tom Van Schaik.

"The whole time I was with them they never got a speeding ticket," he remarks. "We got pulled over half a dozen times, but they always sweet-talked their way out of it. They'd give the officers CDs and pictures and stuff. Sometimes I would be driving when we got pulled over and the officer would be talking to me and—all of a sudden—there would be these three Dixie Chicks heads [in the window] talking to the officer."

Van Schaik chuckles when he thinks about how quickly the Chicks could find their way to the front of the van whenever the police appeared on the scene. "They would always let us go," he says of the police. The only exception he recalls is the time Martie was driving and was pulled over on the Pennsylvania Turnpike.

"They really turned it on for the officer," he says. "But that officer was not about to let them go. After that, Martie didn't drive too much—the fine was a real whopper."

Once, while driving through a thunderstorm, the van was so ravaged by the raging winds that rain started blowing in through the windows. It was so bad that the girls had to grab up their dirty laundry and use it to plug the holes in the van. Emerging from the rainstorm, they realized they had plugged all the windows with a colorful assortment of panties and bras and T-shirts, all of which hung splendidly in full view of other motorists.

One of the most predictable things about being on the road with the Chicks was their eating habits. "A lot of time, when we were in the van, we would have to drive ten or fifteen minutes out of our way so that the girls could eat 'healthy,'" says Van Schaik. "Martie was a vegetarian, so we had to find places that had fresh this and fresh that."

That was fair enough, he says, but there was always a payback at the next stop.

"The next time we filled up with gas, they would come out of the truck stop or service station with Gummi Worms [candy] and Oreos [cookies]. We would go twenty minutes out of our way to eat healthy, and then we would eat Oreos."

Van Schaik savors that thought, allowing it to roll over his lips with, "yuuuuum—brown rice and Gummi Worms!"

In California, they once pulled over at a Denny's restaurant at two in the morning for dinner. "We were sitting around ordering and the waitress came around and one of the girls asked if the shrimp was fresh," says Van Schaik, who cracks up with laughter. "It's two in the morning, and we're at a Denny's. I just looked at her and said, 'Oh, come on.'"

Later, when there were three males traveling with the women—Van Schaik, the guitarist, and soundman, Jeff Humphrey—stopping for food became the high point of the day. "Sometimes it was like an 'I Love Lucy' episode," says Schaik. "They would order something and then they would change the order. I want this, but not this, and I want this on the side. They would break down everything they ordered until it was all on the side.

"Sometimes we'd walk into a restaurant and they would say, 'Oh, a table for six' and we'd say, 'No just break us up into two groups of three. We don't have to sit together.' The guys at one table and the girls, with three special orders, at the other table. We'd always be out of the restaurant before they were."

Back in Dallas that spring, it seemed everything was going their way. They were booked for their first European tour, and they were given an endorsement deal by Justin Boots. It was the first time the Fort Worth-based Texas boot manufacturer had ever given an endorsement deal to an unsigned recording act.

The Chicks were selling more CDs out of the back of their van than many Nashville recording artists were selling with the full promotional clout of major labels.

Interviewed in early 1993 by Tammy Noles of *Trendsetter,* a Texas-based publication, the women listed negotiating a recording contract with a major label as their main goal for the year. Said Laura, "Our motto is 'Pray for a good harvest, but keep on hoein'.'" What appealed most to Emily was that her work allowed her to dispel myths and stereotypes about women: "In my business, women are scarce when it comes to creating the music that's on stage or on a recording. Men dominate the musical virtuosity field at the moment, and I, along with Laura and Martie, love the fact that we are the band as well as the vocalists."

Frustrated by their exploding concert career and their stone-cold dead recording career, the Dixie Chicks decided to discontinue using David Skepner as their manager. Interviewed in 1999, Skepner said he asked the Chicks numerous times why they no longer wanted him to represent them, and their answer was always that they couldn't afford a manager.

"They came to that conclusion on their own, without ever asking me," he says. "They never came to me and said, 'We can't afford to pay you a commission. Could you let it ride a while?' If they had, we would have said, 'Sure, pay us when you can.' But they never asked. It was a decision they came to riding in the back of their van, without any outside forces asking how they thought about this or that. I've asked Laura a couple of times, and I've got the same answer each time."

Despite severing his relationship with the group, Skepner says he has maintained friendships with all of the women. When asked a question that referred to a comment made by Laura, Skepner responded "Laura is just a wonderful human being."

Back on their own again, the Chicks began choosing songs for their next album and packing for their first European tour. "We left with twenty-five pieces of luggage and returned with thirty because we were buying so much stuff," says drummer Van Schaik. "We hauled all those boxes all over Europe."

The Dixie Chicks were booked in Zurich, Switzerland, Monte Carlo, and Brussels, Belgium, where Laura's sister had lived and worked for twenty-one years as a world-class ballerina. It was through her sister's efforts that they got the Brussels booking at a club named Farley's.

In the early 1990s, country music was still lagging behind other American music forms such as blues and rock 'n' roll in Europe. It has since taken a giant stride, perhaps even eclipsing its competitors.

"We played a show there [Farley's] where normal rock bands play, but they have a strong clientele—the owner and the bartender are both musicians," Laura describes. They were also booked at the Thunderbird Cafe in Brussels, the only Mexican restaurant in the city. "NATO is not far out of Brussels, so there is a lot of American personnel in that area," says Laura. "The Thunderbird had a very mixed crowd. There were a lot of homesick Americans there."

While in Brussels, the Chicks went on a shopping spree. Laura attended a street auction and left with chairs, walking canes, and artwork. Emily bought an assortment of perfumes and powder puffs, and she partook of the pastries. Martie, ever the practical one, bought a natty linen suit (there's something deep down inside her that whispers, "bank teller").

To the amusement of the women, the men demonstrated a new category of ways in which the sexes are different. Jeff Humphrey, who doubled as road manager and soundman, packed a suitcase of disposable tube socks and briefs. When he wore them, he simply threw them away. That way, his suitcase lost weight as the trip progressed. Drummer Van

Schaik and guitarist Matthew Benjamin taught the Chicks a new method of recycling. When their laundry bags filled up, they simply turned them over and started at the other end. At least, that's Laura's humorous take on it.

For their sold-out performances in Zurich—"It was called something like Shitenhauzen," says Laura, displaying her customary good humor and doing her best imitation of a Swiss dialect—the Chicks were treated like superstars. "We got our rhinestone garb on and met the mayor, and he gave us an official invitation to the city."

When they returned to Texas, they had to make a decision about what to do about a new album. They were still smarting from the rejections they had received from the major labels for *Little Ol' Cowgirl.* It was an outstanding album, and the group knew it. It was still a big seller for them out on the road, so they knew they would make their money back from a new release.

Recording a new album was not so much a matter of economics or convenience for the Chicks as it was a matter of prestige, or rather the loss of it. Lessor known acts, indeed lesser talented acts, were landing recording contracts with the majors with apparently little effort.

The Chicks knew they had to record a new album. To stop putting new product on the market was tantamount to surrendering their career dreams, and none of them was prepared to do that. Martie called Larry Seyer, who had produced *Little Ol' Cowgirl,* and asked if he was available to produce a new album. Unfortunately, he was booked solid for the next several months. They shopped around and came up with engineer Mike Poole and producer Steve Fishell, a respected guitarist who worked with Jackalope Productions.

Fishell didn't exert the same level of "hands-on" control demonstrated by Seyer, so the Chicks did most of the preproduction work themselves, which by now they were more than willing to undertake. They decided to title the album, *Shouldn't a Told You That,* after one of the singles written by Mike Hiatt. The song had been recorded for them on a home recorder by a friend.

The band liked the song and added it to their live act. Says Laura, "Whenever someone gave us a song [to consider] and the group gave a thumbs up to, we'd take notice of [it]." Thus, "Shouldn't a Told You That" went to the top of the heap by virtue of what their live audiences seemed to like.

They chose a second song, "Whistles and Bells," after its cowriter

Radney Foster called them and sang it to them over the telephone. At that time, Foster was being touted as one of the breakout new artists of the 1990s, so just getting a call from him was a thrill.

Another song, "There Goes My Dream," was written by Jamie O'Hara, who as a member of the critically acclaimed duet, the O'Kanes, had broken new ground in country music in the late 1980s. The O'Kanes had a sparse, acoustic sound and intricate harmonies that gave their music a bluesy attitude.

Also contributing to the album was legendary songwriter Jim Lauderdale. His "Planet of Love," a ballad that allowed the girls to demonstrate what they could do with harmony, was a good vehicle for Laura's honey-rich voice and nerve-jangling sense of timing (she can push a song right to the edge, then pause just long enough to make you think she has missed her reentry, then jump back in without missing a beat).

Thrown into that mix were two songs cowritten by guitarist Matthew Benjamin. "One Heart Away," was created with drummer Tom Van Schaik, while "I'm Falling Again," was co-penned with Laura, Martie, and Emily. A third in-house song was "The Thrill Is in the Chase," a song written by Laura and Dave Peters.

The highlight of the album may be Martie's lead vocal on "I Wasn't Looking for You." It is the only known recording in which she ever stepped up front and sang lead. Her voice is a bit thin, as you might expect—a thinness that derived as much from the case of nerves it gave her as from her natural voice—but it provided the song with the proper tension and will probably make that particular album a collector's edition.

"We didn't know what we wanted musically," Laura says. "We didn't want to stay too traditional bluegrass. We wanted to give people something new to listen to. We had fun doing it, but we probably didn't do a real wise job picking songs. By the time we came in off the road and got into the studio, we were pooped out. It would have been nice to have had the luxury of having some good songwriters pitching us songs."

Finishing work on an album is supposed to be a joyous experience. However, the fact of the matter is that it is tiring, hard work that leaves everyone involved riddled with self-doubt and bouts of exhaustion that are sometimes difficult to shake for weeks thereafter. The good news was that no one in Nashville sent word to them that they hated the new album. The bad news was that no one liked it well enough to sign them to a recording contract.

These near-miss recording sessions were becoming like daggers to their hearts. The Dixie Chicks did everything they could think of to attract attention to themselves.

Once, they managed to get themselves booked as an opening act at a Reba McEntire concert they had heard would be attended by MCA Records head Tony Brown. Sure enough, the legendary record executive was in the audience.

"We thought, 'He's gonna love this,'" recalls Laura. "We were so excited! We had these big rubber smiles glued on our faces from ear to ear. We looked like cartoon characters, and that's what he told people later—'they're too cartoony'—which I thought was so funny. But, at the time, we were crushed. We didn't want to be cartoon characters. We wanted to be real."

A Texas newspaper music critic once attacked the Chicks for much the same reason. When the Chicks heard the critic would be attending their show, they were elated.

"We gave him the best seats in the house," recalls Laura. "We gave him our best burritos and our best conversation. When he left, we thought, 'Well, we finally won him over.' But no! The next day, he described us as 'painfully happy.' He said it made his cheeks hurt to watch us. He slaughtered us and it made us so depressed."

By the fall of 1994, the Dixie Chicks knew they were going to have to reach deeply into their pockets to finance the release of *Shouldn't a Told You That*. Like all the other albums, it would be manufactured and distributed by Crystal Clear Sound of Dallas. The company would turn out the disks for a fee, then work to get them distributed in retail outlets that would accept product from indies.

Commenting on the release of the new CD in their fall newsletter, the Dixie Chicks hyped the new product under a headline that asked, "Is the third time the charm?" Said the newsletter: "The newspapers and music writers are saying we're getting back to our 'country roots'—when did we ever leave? Then there's talk about Nashville lovin' it. What does all this mean?"

The question was not rhetorical. It was an expression of frustration. The only thing comparable would be for a politician to constantly receive compliments that he is doing a great job, then to be defeated at the polls by the same people who had voiced support for him.

Announcing the release of their third album, the newsletter said the Chicks "got to get all duded-up with fancy makeup artists and lots of primin' and backgrounds (a far jump from shooting our pictures against Laura's bedroom wall.) . . . The real kicker is the fact that we now go into the studio with comfortable pillows, bowls of fruit and shoes that don't hurt our feet."

Shouldn't a Told You That was released at a big party on November 11, 1994, at the Granada Theater in Dallas. Wrote Laura in the newsletter, "There were probably a hundred record company scouts out there, but we can only see to the fifth row—so don't spoil our illusion."

NATALIE CIRCLES THE BAIT LIKE A SLEEPY OL' CATFISH

1994

A *fter* two semesters at West Texas A&M, Natalie Maines enrolled at South Plains College in Levelland, Texas, in the fall of 1993. By then she was very much aware of the Dixie Chicks and of her dad's growing association with the group.

"I had met her once or twice by then," says drummer Tom Van Schaik. "When the Chicks played Lubbock, Lloyd came out and did some of the bigger shows. Afterward, we'd always go over to Lloyd's house, and his wife, Tina, would cook a big meal. Natalie was usually there. She was just this kid running around the house."

Laura Lynch recalls Natalie attending the shows when they played Lubbock, sometimes showing up with her sister, Kim, and she recalls the family dinners the Chicks enjoyed with Lloyd and Tina, but she doesn't recall Natalie demonstrating any special interest in the band, at least not in 1994.

"She's twenty years younger than me," says Laura in the way of an explanation. If you had asked Natalie at that time if she had any interest in someday becoming a member of the Dixie Chicks she probably would have responded with an exaggerated "YEAH, DAH." Her musical tastes went in another direction.

The influence that Lloyd exerted over Natalie's choice of South Plains is probably known only to father and daughter, but there is little doubt that it conformed to a father's perception of what was best for his daughter. South Plains College is only a short distance from the Maines household in Lubbock. Because Natalie had a little bit of the rebel in her, Papa may have wanted her where he could keep a watchful eye on her. Of course, Natalie soon found reasons of her own to appease her dad. At South Plains she met and fell in love with Michael Tarabay, who would later become her husband. Both were students at the college and both were on parallel quests for self-identity. Both saw music as the key to whatever lay in store for them in life.

South Plains offers a commercial music program that is one of the largest of its kind in the world. It awards associate degrees in commercial music and is the only college in Texas that offers a degree in country and bluegrass music.

The school's multimillion-dollar facility boasts four recording studios, a television studio, and five rehearsal halls. Some of its former students include country artists Lee Ann Womack; Heath Wright, lead singer for the country group Richochet; and Mike Bub, winner of the International Bluegrass Music Association Award of 1997 for "Bass Player of the Year."

"South Plains College was the best thing I ever did for my career," Lee Ann Womack told the Levelland and Hockley County *New Press* in 1997. (The singer spent a year at the college studying country music before heading to Nashville in 1990. Her first single, "Never Again, Again," cracked the Top 10 the first week it was issued.) "For the first time in my life, I was totally surrounded by music, by people who loved music the way I did. I spent every day at South Plains working on music."

The school has a reputation for doing the impossible, which is to say teaching students the basics of achieving a career in music. One of its music instructors is Cary Banks, a former member of the Maines Brothers Band.

"Natalie took piano from me every semester she was here," says Banks who joined the staff as an instructor in 1993 and quickly became the coordinator of the school's commercial music program. "She was mostly into rock 'n' roll, rhythm and blues. She wanted to learn the old jazz stuff and new James Taylor, Lenny Kravitz, or Janet Jackson. Especially alternative styles of rock."

Banks has known Natalie since she was "a day old." He says he never saw her show an interest in music as a career until she enrolled at South Plains. "I had watched her develop over the years, so I knew she had the personality [to go into music]," he says. "In her case, it was a combination of genetics and environment coming together. We have ensemble classes and the classes perform on stage and they are filmed before a live audience and broadcast before a cable audience here at the school.

"When I saw her [on film], I knew then she was going to be a star. She has that charisma you don't see too often. It just turned on when she got on stage. Offstage, she's not shy, but she is not especially outgoing. She was always an individual. She never dressed like anyone else. She never fit in, or so she thought."

When Banks' children, Katie and Cody, were two and three years of age, Natalie was their baby-sitter. "When the Dixie Chicks' first video came out [in 1998], Katie and Cody happened to have some of their friends over watching television," Banks recalls. "Katie says, 'Look! That used to be my baby-sitter!' and her friends were like, 'No way!'"

Banks always enjoyed encountering Natalie on campus because it seemed she was always getting into some kind of mischief and needing to vent a little steam. "She would get into a lot of political arguments," he recalls. "She was a big fan of [Texas Governor] Ann Richards. Well, a lot of instructors are dyed-in-the-wool Republicans, and one in particular loved to tease her about it.

"Once she had a crush on one of her guitar instructors, and she was teased about that. She took exception to that, but it was obvious [to everyone] she had a crush on him.

"I think she really liked parts of being a student, but I don't think she cared for the academic environment. She's always been opinionated and hardheaded like her dad. She didn't have too much to do with many of the students out here. She had one little pack [of people] she ran with, but she didn't do much socializing. She lived on campus one semester. The other semesters she lived with a female friend in an apartment."

By the end of 1994, Natalie had apparently had enough of South Plains. In December, she went to New Orleans to audition for a vocal scholarship with Berklee's "North American Scholarship Tour." She was ready to be all she could be.

In March 1994 the Dixie Chicks packed up their bags and headed back to Europe.

Armed with an official proclamation from Dallas Mayor Steve Bartlett naming the Dixie Chicks the city's Official Music Ambassadors to Europe, they played two sold-out concerts in Zurich, Switzerland, then moved on to EuroDisney near Paris, where they performed for three nights at Billy Bob's authentic Texas-style saloon.

"We were such a novelty in Paris," Laura recalls. "The sound systems were usually terrible, but they gave us presents and in their broken English told us the nicest things."

It was while they were performing at EuroDisney, remembers drummer Tom Van Schaik, that Laura began losing her voice temporarily because of the frequency with which she was performing. "We had to keep the stage volume really soft, but even that was not enough. I went next door to a restaurant and got some day-old breadsticks to use in the place of my drumsticks. No one noticed until I took a bite out of one of them."

One morning, they toured the Eiffel Tower. On the elevator ride up with a group of Moroccan tourists, the Chicks startled everyone by breaking out into a hee-haw version of the "Star-Spangled Banner."

That evening in Paris, they performed at the New Morning, a famous club venue that had been frequented by jazz trumpeter Miles Davis. Recalls Van Schaik in astonishment: "My major at North Texas University was in jazz studies. I walked in and saw all these billboards of Miles Davis and John Coltrane, and I thought, 'OK, now we've got the Dixie Chicks next to Miles Davis. There's something wacky about this.'"

Before their performance at the New Morning, the Dixie Chicks participated in a radio interview with Nina Hagen, a former East German singer who was noted for her radical politics. The Chicks did not know what to expect from Hagen, so they began asking her questions. The best defense, went the Chicks credo, is a good offense.

"What do you think is the reason for the newfound popularity of country music?" one of the Chicks inquired, playing the role of the radio interviewer.

Hagen gave them the best European answer she could muster. "Country music has been and always will be what it is," she sniffed.

The Dixie Chicks could relate to that.

In Monte Carlo, their last stop of the tour, their hosts offered prizes for the most authentic western outfits and asked the Chicks to judge the contest. "There's nothing quite like a French Riviera cowboy—spurs on penny loafers and cardigans with chaps," said the girls in their newsletter. "They are still in love with Sue Ellen and J. R. Ewing."

The women spent their last evening with a bottle of "Chateau de

Chugalug" and toasted their trip with a pledge to leave Chick tracks in Moscow on their next overseas trip.

Just when it looked like it could not possibly get any better for the group, Robin reentered the picture. Since leaving the Dixie Chicks, she had formed an alliance with singer/guitarist Sara Hickman and Patty Lege of the bluegrass group Red Oak.

Although Hickman continued to perform solo and Lege continued to perform with Red Oak, they formed a trio with Robin which they named the Domestic Science Club. It was sort of a watered-down version of the Dixie Chicks, in that it offered the Earth Mama persona in triplicate, bluegrass without the glitter and makeup.

"There was some bad blood," Tom Van Schaik recalls. "When [Robin] left, she actually tried to take the name of the group with her. She went through the whole lawsuit process. It was a major, major time in the history of the band. It could have easily ended everything. I remember one time they [Laura, Martie, and Emily] were scratching their heads wondering if it was worth pursuing.

"It was a disruption in what was going on because the girls had to deal with lawyers. Robin wanted . . . residuals on what she had done. The girls didn't have any problem with paying residuals. They weren't going to give her any future earnings. They felt that anything from that point on was going to be theirs."

The "bad blood" reached its peak in February 1994, when Robin filed a petition against her former bandmates in a Dallas County court, alleging that they had not lived up to the 1992 agreement. Robin charged them with breach of contract and with fraud and asked for a judgment of at least one hundred thousand dollars.

By mid-February, Robin and her former bandmates had resolved all their difficulties, and the court dismissed the complaint on the grounds that all the issues had been settled. When push had come to pull, the women returned to the standards set forth in their "pinkie pull." As is customary in American state and federal courts, the terms of settlement are not afforded the same public access as are the complaints made in the lawsuit.

By this point, the guys in the band almost would have paid to tour with the group.

"I used to have all these sound guys backstage, loading equipment, doing sound checks, come up to me and say, 'You mean you get to look at this every night?'" says drummer Van Schaik. "I was like, yeah . . . they'd say, 'How much can we pay you?' But to me, it was like looking at my sister. I was married at the time and had no interest in any relationship with anyone in the band. But it was pretty interesting traveling with them. Like any band out on the road you're going to have your disagreements. Times when someone needs their space. It's like a brother–sister thing. You're mad one minute and the next you're not."

Conversation aboard the van didn't deviate too far from the business at hand. Mostly the girls talked about the music industry, but sometimes they took turns asking everyone what they thought about their current boyfriends. Laughs Van Schaik, "We didn't discuss things like Kosovo [current political events of the day]."

Occasionally, Laura allowed her daughter, Asia, to accompany them on road trips. One of those treks was to a concert where the Dixie Chicks opened for country singer Ricky Van Shelton, who was in the midst of a string of hits dating back to the late 1980s.

"It was a lot of fun riding in the RV to that concert," Asia recollects. At the time of the trip Asia was in the sixth grade. "It was like a group of high school girlfriends playing dress up and singing. They were silly on the RV and made jokes. Everyone was funny. My mom is like the pun queen. They told lots of silly jokes. They were funny because they were so corny."

When they arrived at the venue, Asia was taken backstage to meet Ricky Van Shelton. "When they went on, I had my own table right up front by the stage, and I had a little security guard sitting with me," Asia recalls.

Everyone always made a big deal about having Asia around. She was, after all, the only Baby Chick (and still holds that distinction). "I was always played with and passed around," she says. "Everything they got for the band, I got a little one of. Like, they had band jackets from Justin Boots [the company that provided them with boots and jackets and sometimes used their photos in print ads], and I got a little jacket just like theirs. I got pampered from every direction. Everyone always heard so much about me from my mom, I think they thought I was a plaything they could play with."

On another occasion, the Dixie Chicks went to El Paso to perform at the rodeo. Asia was taken backstage to meet everyone and proceeded to dazzle them with some new skills she had acquired. "I had learned a whole lot of new magic card tricks," she says. "I did them for everyone, and they pretended to be mesmerized. They thought it was really cool. I only had one trick mastered, and it was a no-brainer. I could make a card float up out of the deck, and it was like a foolproof trick, but everyone loved it."

Growing up as the only Baby Chick was not always fun and games. There were moments when Asia missed her mother and wished she were at home with her all the time. "I didn't have the feeling of, like, I was torn up about it every day," says Asia. "There were times when I would cry because I missed her. But that was an unusual thing. I thought it was a cool thing she was doing. None of the other girls and boys in my class had a parent who was doing that. I did miss her a lot, more so at some times than at other times. But it was a lot of fun when she came to town. We would pick right up where we left off last time."

Once the Dixie Chicks were passing through Detroit in their van in the middle of the night. Laura was at the wheel, and everyone else was sound asleep (the band members took turns at the wheel). Suddenly, the van lurched left to right, as if the vehicle were making wide sweeps.

"I woke up and saw that I was being thrown around in the back of the van," says drummer Van Schaik. "Laura was going, like, sixty-five miles per hour through this construction zone. I said, 'Laura, Laura, hit the brakes!'"

When the van slowed down, Van Schaik asked Laura what had happened. "She said, 'Well, I didn't want to take off the cruise control.'" Van Schaik told Laura that he would drive the rest of the way if she would pull over at the next exit. "Those are the times," he muses, "when you are thinking, 'Now why did I get myself into this?'"

The women would occasionally allow one of their boyfriends to drive. "We had this one guy who did some driving for us," says Van Schaik. "One night I was in the passenger seat and looked over and realized the driver was sound asleep. His head was bobbing up and down like one of those little dogs in the back of a car.

"One other time this same guy was driving when we were leaving the parking lot of a nightclub. He hooked the bumper of a pickup truck and drove off and ripped the bumper off the pickup and bent our bumper."

Not all the moments on the road with the Chicks were nerve-shattering.

Before going on to do a show, the Chicks used their van as a launching pad for their nervous energies and fantasies. One of their staple rituals was something they called the Dance Party. "We'd put on Donna Summer or Marvin Gaye on the boom box in the van or in the dressing room, and everyone—no matter how pissy they felt—had to do a 'move' of some sort," Laura remembers.

So, there the Chicks are, moments before going on to sing the "Star-Spangled Banner," or moments before performing at a music festival, and they are in the back of their van, shaking, shimmying, and rocking like cheerleaders, or vamping like strippers trying to work up a Saturday night crowd of guys, all in the name of girl-power motivation. "Before we had to go on and smile to the crowd, we had to feel happy," she says. "It worked. Maybe it's another one of those girl things."

One of the constant frustrations out on the road was male technicians who didn't want to give the women musicians credit for their musical talents. Once, at a showcase for a fair buyers' convention in Nashville, Van Schaik went through the system with the sound guys, telling them what to plug in for sound.

"At the end of the show one of the guys I knew at the convention came up and said none of the girls' instruments were plugged in," Van Schaik recalls. "I said, 'What!' He said, 'Yeah, you can't hear the fiddle or the banjo.' I went up there to talk to the soundman, and he told me he thought the girls were just holding props. He thought that since they were just up there for looks there was no point in plugging them into the PA system. They battled that for years, just gaining respect for their instruments."

On another occasion, they were playing in Alabama, opening for Ronnie Milsap. All during sound check they felt like something was wrong, says Laura. "We knew that there was something not big [experienced musicians can often 'see' the way their music fills a room] out there. We asked them to turn off all the monitors, and we played without them. We had lead guitar and drums out front. Everything else was turned off. We went to the sound man and said, 'You've got to turn it on.'

"The soundman said, 'Oh, you mean they work? They're plugged in—and everything?'"

Simon Renshaw is not a music expert, and he'd probably be the first to tell you that. What he does profess an expertise in is money. That's because his background is as an accountant. When he came to the United

States from his native Great Britain, it was to make a name for himself as an accountant and not as a music mogul. He ended up working for Lone Wolf Management of Houston (later of Austin), Texas. Most folks outside the industry have never heard of Lone Wolf Management, but they are probably aware of the management firm's biggest client, ZZ Top.

ZZ Top rose to stardom with several hard-driving guitar licks, which the band faithfully duplicates in a variety of ways, and a visual mystique enhanced by bushy, navel-length beards that shroud their identity. If you buy the beat and buy the look, then you've bought the band. There's no rocket science involved.

By 1974, the three-piece band had been crisscrossing the United States for five years, doing one one-nighter after another—and had nothing to show for it. By chance that year, they performed at the Memphis Blues Show, a low-paying venue for blues and blues-rock musicians.

While in Memphis, the group stopped by Ardent Recording, a state-of-the art recording facility begun by Memphis businessman John Fry with the help of his childhood friend and later business associate, Frederick Smith (the founder of Federal Express). The members of ZZ Top were so impressed with the studio that they made arrangements to record their next album there.

In the years since, ZZ Top has made very few recordings that were not done in Memphis. As the band's recording time in Memphis increased, so did the percentage of its finances that passed through the Bluff City (they don't call it that for nothing). What Renshaw discovered when he began working for Lone Wolf Productions was a financial system in place in Memphis that was even more impressive than the music generated by the musicians in the Memphis studios.

Music groups, like many other businesses, hire accountants to look after their money. That means collecting it from venues where they perform, from T-shirt vendors, record companies, music performance associations such as ASCAP and BMI, and a host of other sources. Often the funds arrive in cash.

Once they collect the money, it is the accountant's job to move it around in ways that will most benefit the clients. Memphis is not only the birthplace of the blues and rock 'n' roll, it is the birthplace of most of the creative accounting techniques now associated with the music business. Renshaw learned a great deal about the industry through his experiences in Memphis.

By the 1990s, Simon Renshaw and Lone Wolf had a parting of the ways. Country artist Clint Black, who had signed with Lone Wolf back in the 1980s, wanted his freedom from the management company. Renshaw ended up leaving his job at Lone Wolf to represent Black until he found another manager.

Once he got Black squared away with new management, Renshaw moved to Nashville, where he started up his own company, Senior Management. One of Renshaw's first clients was Jamie O'Hara, who submitted a song for the Dixie Chicks' most recent album.

It was in the summer of 1994 that Renshaw first met the Chicks. It had been about a year since the Chicks had a manager and, with the release of *Shouldn't a Told You That* a few months earlier, they were sensing that they needed to do something drastic, careerwise, to keep the group afloat.

In a special section in its "Unsigned Artists and Regional News Section" for early June, *Billboard* magazine published a few paragraphs about the success the Dixie Chicks were having without a "commercially accepted" sound.

"Our strength is in songs we engage the audience in live," Laura told the trade magazine. "Record labels want something we're not. We think we're about to hit a happy medium [with *Shouldn't a Told You That*]."

The biggest surprise of the summer was a letter Laura received from "Ripley's Believe It Or Not" that her bass, which was shaped like a huge saguaro cactus, had been chosen for mention in its "Believe It Or Not" newspaper column. That was a real surprise . . . well, a hoot actually. But it raised questions about whether that was the direction the band really wanted to go.

Enter Simon Renshaw. He was an outsider, like the Chicks, someone who didn't seem to fit in with the good old boys of country music. He has an affected way about him, one that wouldn't raise an eyebrow in Europe, but one that earmarked him as an outsider in Nashville.

Renshaw was recommended to the Chicks by Paul Lohr at Buddy Lee Attractions, the booking agency that kept the Chicks on the road. Booking agencies do just that—book performances. They do not otherwise get involved in an artist's career. Lohr apparently felt the Chicks needed some career guidance.

When the girls met Renshaw, they were impressed by the way he looked, and they felt his British accent added a touch a class to their presentation. "I don't even want to manage you if you're not on a label, but I can probably get you on a label," he told the girls, according to Laura. "Is that OK?"

The girls swooned.

"He was pretty cocky from the beginning, and we took that as 'Wow, we're lucky to have him,' and that British accent, that bossiness," Laura explains. "We thought, 'He's really a busy man about town.' We jumped on it one hundred percent. We thought, 'Yeah, we've done a great thing for ourselves.'"

Renshaw was true to his word. No sooner did they sign with him on July 1, 1994, than he went to Blake Chancey, vice president of artists and repertoire at Sony Records, and returned with a plan to record the Dixie Chicks for that record label. Chancey himself would be the producer of the album.

The Dixie Chicks could hardly believe their good fortune.

All that changed when, at the end of his first month as their manager, Renshaw sent the Dixie Chicks a bill for $11,654.55 for his services, according to Laura. "We about died when we saw the statement," Laura says. "That's when I started discussing the fancy rental cars [he was using] and the lamb chops and room service at the Radisson suite while we were staying in Motel 6. We paid those statements, but it was painful and we each took a reduction in pay to do it."

Their flamboyant manager taught the Chicks two valuable lessons: Never take anything for granted in the music business, and never, never allow a manager to have an unlimited expense account. The Chicks must have felt like firing Renshaw over the incident, but they didn't, for by that time they were already in too deep with him.

That fall, in what the Chicks interpreted as a sign of better things to come, they awoke to find a photo of Laura and Emily with Texas billionaire and presidential candidate Ross Perot on the front page of the *New York Times* (September 12, 1994). In the photograph, Laura and Emily were laughing at something Perot had said, and the billionaire was leaning over toward Emily. Next to the photo of the Chicks was one of actress Jessica Tandy, who had died of cancer at the age of eighty-five.

If being on the front page of the *New York Times* with Ross Perot and Jessica Tandy was not proof that the Dixie Chicks were finally on the right professional track, what could possibly satisfy the critics—and their own nagging inner doubts?

LAURA'S SURPRISE RETIREMENT PARTY

1995

The Dixie Chicks were ready to let their hair down, Martie especially.

They began 1995 by performing at the inauguration of Texas Governor George W. Bush. Said the Chicks of the event in their newsletter: "Lots of shakers and movers and plenty of regular folks like us too. We were all in the Austin Convention Center for hours of horse d'oovers [sic], dancing and chasing news crews for coverage."

From there it was on to the Hard Rock Cafe in Dallas and, over the next several months, a string of performances across Texas and occasional trips to North Carolina and Tennessee.

As they traveled around the country, they experienced an Elvis sighting at the Gator Lounge in Lake Charles, Louisiana, purchased a rear differential from the Crow Indians in Wyoming, and, with Emily at the wheel, got pulled over for an illegal U-turn. When Emily tried to bribe the police officer with their latest CD, he told her that would not work with him. "I already have all three," he said.

On their way to Butte, Montana, they kept seeing roadside signs for a post-branding "Testicle Festival" and horseshoe throwing contest. Figuring that was one event where they would fit right in, they tried to find the location, but were unsuccessful. The girls said they were sure everyone there had a ball.

Martie's life, in particular, was changing. She had fallen in love with Ted Ashley Seidel, a twenty-nine-year-old pharmaceutical salesman who was raising a young son, Carter, from a previous marriage. Seidel was a regular guy who had proved his dedication to his son. Equally important to Martie, he was not involved in the music business.

Born in Sioux City, Iowa, Seidel moved to Texas in 1995. Although not a Southerner, his middle name "Ashley" had a *Gone with the Wind* identification to it, which cast him in a romantic light. Martie felt that if push came to shove, Ted would stick with her, no matter what. Martie and Ted set a wedding date of June 17, 1995.

One of the first things Simon Renshaw did as the Dixie Chicks new manager was to prepare a four-minute promotional video. It blended concert footage with video clips from television appearances, and it featured original interviews with band members.

In one of the interviews (which were usually ten to twenty seconds in duration), Laura said they received a letter from a radio station in Hawaii. "The morning drive guy said you are the most requested country band in Hawaii—who are you?"

The girls thought that was funny.

The announcer on the video described the Dixie Chicks as "three young women with looks, brains and a heck of a lot of talent" who have "come a long ways since the days they sang on a downtown Dallas street corner for spare change." With a combination of down-home country and urban glamour, continued the announcer, "the Dixie Chicks are three Texas women living a honky-tonk dream."

In another interview, the women were asked if they were ready for stardom. "We're ready for the next level, I think," said Laura. "I don't know what stardom is."

The video said the women had a grassroots following that had spread across the country. As proof, it flashed a series of photographs across the screen showing the women with a variety of celebrities, including entertainer Liza Minnelli, talk show host Larry King, and Dallas Cowboys quarterback Troy Aikman.

At that time, one of the best venues for unsigned talent was *Music City Tonight* with Crook and Chase, which aired on the Nashville Network (TNN). Hosts Lorianne Crook and Charlie Chase had a long history of giving breaks to unsigned talent. Not only did this place the hosts in an advocative role for deserving entertainers, it was good public relations for the show and provided their studio audience with fresh live entertainment.

On the April 6, 1995, telecast of *Music City Tonight,* the Dixie Chicks were booked with Grand Ole Opry star Johnny Russell and comedian Killer Beaz. Wearing jeans and informal western wear—their retro-cowgirl costumes were, by that time, relegated to state fairs and the like—the Dixie Chicks performed a Bobbie Gentry-style song entitled "Jump on It," after which they joined Crook and Chase on the TV set for a little conversation.

Chase told them he had seen something that day while sitting out on the "front porch" that disturbed him. "I saw the most unusual thing involving their motor home," he told the audience. Then, while the Chicks froze in panic like deer caught in the headlights of an oncoming car, Chase reached out for Martie's hand, explaining that he wanted her to go outside with him.

Martie seemed reluctant. "I don't think so," she answered.

"Come on," urged Chase, refusing to take no for an answer.

After Martie and Chase disappeared off the set, Laura and Emily glanced at each other, as the void on the sofa where Martie had been sitting grew larger and larger. With Charlie and Martie gone, Lorianne picked up the conversation.

"Who knows what he's talking about?" asked Lorianne.

Laura and Emily looked at each like pickpockets who had been busted.

"We've heard that things sometimes haven't been going well on tour, technically," said Lorianne. "What's been happening, Laura?"

Emily glanced at Laura, horror-struck.

"This year, one of our biggest bloopers was falling through the stage in Muleshoe, Texas, during a song," said Laura. "I was up to about here [motioning to her neck], just a singing head on stage."

Lorianne cut them off, allowing the director to go to an outside camera.

Martie and Charlie were outside in the parking lot, standing next to the Chicks' RV.

"This is the motor home that the Dixie Chicks travel in," Chase informed the audience.

Martie gasped, holding her hands over her face.

"You know what I'm talking about now, don't you?"

"Everybody thought we were in a bus . . ."

"No, this is a very nice motor home. When I looked out this afternoon, the problem was you couldn't get in it, right?"

Martie explained that they had locked the keys in the RV.

"Show them how you opened it."

"Are you serious?"

"Oh, yes."

"You're the gentleman here," Martie said, asking if she could hoist him through the window.

"No, I'm a television host. You go up there and show them how you got in."

"I'm gonna need your help, Charlie."

"What do you want me to do?"

Martie stood outside the RV window, trying to figure out what to do next.

Charlie pointed to a pickup truck parked next to the RV, instructing her to step up into the truck. Like a true gentleman, Chase pulled down the tailgate of the truck. Martie took his hand and stepped up into the truck. First, she tried to enter the window of the RV headfirst, kicking her perky behind up into the air for all of televisionland to admire. Then, sensing that the camera may be zooming in on her posterior, she thought better of that position and entered the RV feetfirst through the window.

"Don't worry about the fact that you're on national television doing this," said Charlie, playfully tormenting his guest.

Moments later she disappeared into the window and then emerged from the door.

"Didn't she do a great job?" said Charlie, giving the audience the high sign.

As Martie and Charlie returned to the studio, the camera switched back to Lorianne, who asked Laura and Emily why Martie was the one who had to crawl in the window when the keys were locked inside.

"When we lock the keys in, we have to take turns," answered Laura. "The three guys never lock them in. One of us always locks them in."

"Does this happen a lot?"

"Things like this happen all the time," said Emily.

Lorianne said she wanted to know more about the stage in Texas that Laura mentioned earlier.

"Actually, it was built out of hay bales. It was a great stage; it worked wonderfully. I just found the one hole in it and went on down in there."

As they were talking, Chase and Martie returned to the TV set.

"It wasn't me who locked the keys in the RV," said Martie. "It was Emily."

"Oh, no," said Emily, standing up for herself.

Lorianne told the audience that Martie was getting married, then she asked Laura if she was available.

"I'm divorced, yeah."

"So do we put up an 800 number now or something?" deadpanned Charlie.

Before the show ended, Charlie, who is known for the good-natured ribbing he sometimes dishes out to his guests, made it clear to Martie that it was all in fun: "I just wanted you to know, Martie, that I would have liked to have helped out, but this is not the proper wardrobe for breaking and entering."

"Yeah, yeah, yeah," said Martie, breaking into a smile.

After winning the vocal scholarship at Berklee College of Music, Natalie Maines enrolled for the spring 1995 session and relocated to Boston. The school features two programs: one that offers a degree and another that offers a diploma.

Natalie chose the less restrictive diploma program. She wasn't sure what she wanted to do with her life, only that Berklee seemed to be the next step.

Despite published reports that she flunked out, Berklee officials say Natalie did quite well in her courses. Upon completing her studies, she returned to Lubbock and enrolled in Texas Tech University for the June–July summer semester. She took only one course—"Introductory Wildlife."

If there were ever a college course designed for students who want to bide their time, it would have to be "Introductory Wildlife." Even so, according to Michael Sommermeyer in the public relations department at the university, Natalie did quite well in the course.

By the time Natalie left Berklee, the Dixie Chicks had been under contract with manager Simon Renshaw for almost one year. On June 16, 1995, while Natalie was attending Texas Tech, the Chicks saw a six-year dream come true: They signed a recording contract with Sony Records, the result of Renshaw's contacts at the record label. After all these years, they were finally going to get a taste of the Big Time. That evening, the Chicks celebrated both the recording contract and Martie's impending wedding.

*   *   *

Wearing a white, low-cut cotton dress cinched at the waist with a pink ribbon, sheer white stockings, and a three-flower bridal bouquet in her hair, which she had pulled up onto the top of her head, Martie looked every bit the bride in her pseudo wedding gown. With her were her lovely bridesmaids, including her two sisters, Emily and Julia.

The women sat together on a padded bench. No sooner did they order a bottle of champagne, than the music began. A hard-thumping bass beat rumbled beneath the music. The Dixie Chicks were in no church, that was certain.

The crowded bench the women shared was at LaBare, Dallas's premier "ladies only" nightclub. Martie watched as the first of several male strippers, wearing only a G-string, danced out into the spotlight. Martie and her wedding party were seated in the "pit," a sunken area near the stage, a favorite spot for bachelorette parties.

Randy Ricks was there that night, working as a dancer. Three years later, he would own LaBare, but on that night he was just another working dancer, the spitting image of a bronco-bustin' cowboy. Having the Dixie Chicks in the club wasn't that big of a deal to the dancers, he says, since they were considered a local band. "But if they came into the club now, it would be, like, the biggest day of their lives for some of the guys," he says. "I really respect those girls for what they have done. People around here really respect them . . . forgive me for saying this, but they could shit on stage and people here would go crazy."

Martie was the guest of honor, so the male dancers focused their attention on her, knowing that she was there for one last fling. They gathered around her, flattering her, treating her like a queen. Of course, it didn't hurt that, for most of the night, she held a fistful of dollars that she tucked, one at a time, into the dancers' G-strings. "She was just having fun," says a woman who was there.

Occasionally, Martie got carried away and ran her hands over the dancers' well-muscled chests. As the evening wore on, Martie's bridesmaids seemed to stiffen somewhat amid the sexual fireworks display taking place around them, especially when one of the dancers pressed his legs between the would-be bride's outstretched knees.

When one of the strippers, a blonde body builder with short hair, pressed Martie's wrists against the back of the bench to remove a dollar bill from her mouth with his lips, the bridesmaids burst into laughter.

Later, as the dancers straddled Martie's lap and became more suggestive in their movements, the discomfort clearly showed on the bridesmaids' faces. At one point, Martie looped her arms around the bullish neck of one of the strippers and, from a distance, appeared to be making out with him.

The climax of the evening occurred when two dancers placed Martie between them, transforming her into a Dixie Chick sandwich. One dancer held her hands up over her head as he gyrated his pelvis against her, while the other dancer pressed his pectoral muscles into her face. Not particularly disturbed by her sister's flirtations was Emily, who captured every amorous moment on film, as did several other photographers.

Ricks says there was nothing unusual about Martie's party. Bachelorette parties comprise sixty percent of his business, so there is almost always one going on in the club. "Of course, the girls always lie about where they've been," he says with a laugh.

Ricks, a former *Playgirl* centerfold (February 1997), has danced for many female country music stars, including Tanya Tucker and Dottie West. Once the Spice Girls showed up outside the club in their tour bus, but they had to be turned away because the club was simply too packed for the women and their entourage of sixty to be seated.

In the mid-1990s, Ricks and the Dixie Chicks often performed at the same clubs. While the women sang and played their instruments, he stripped and danced for the ladies in the audience. Says Ricks, "The Dixie Chicks are all as sweet as can be. They're all dolls."

Of course, Martie had more than one merger to celebrate that night. Martie, Emily, and Laura had signed a recording contract with Sony Records earlier in the day. All of their dreams were about to come true. How often does a woman sign a recording contract and attend her bachelorette party on the same day?

The following day—June 17, 1995—Martie walked down the aisle of St. Luke's Episcopal Church in Dallas, accompanied by the same group of bridesmaids who had stood up for her in LaBare. Nowhere to be seen were the LaBare dancers.

Martie wore a traditional white gown for the ceremony, which was held in a church-in-the-round setting, with the couple standing at the pulpit in the center of the church. By that time, Martie's parents had divorced and both were remarried. Giving away the bride were Mr. and

Mrs. Farrell Trask, Martie's mother and new husband, and Mr. and Mrs. Paul Erwin, her father and his new wife.

"It was a very traditional, straitlaced wedding," recalls Dallas music store owner Jay Rury, who attended the wedding with his wife, Shelley. "It was not cowboy-cowgirl oriented. There was music from the choir. It went like any wedding would go. The reception afterward was at a swanky club, the top floor of a high rise. That was very nice, very traditional. They had a DJ playing music."

Over the next several months, Blake Chancey, vice president of artists and repertoire at Sony Nashville, changed professional hats and went into the studio to produce several songs with the Dixie Chicks. It is not unheard of for A&R executives to produce albums for artists on the company roster, but it is not encouraged because it can give the appearance of a conflict of interest. When executives wear both hats they are obligated, ethically at least, not to receive income directly from any source other than the record company itself.

Exactly how many songs Chancey recorded with the Chicks over the summer has remained a closely guarded company secret. It is known that none of the songs that were put on tape were what the record company was looking for. So Chancey kept trying.

Meanwhile, Martie and Emily cowrote a song, "You Were Mine," which they thought had merit. Earlier in the year, while Natalie was attending Berklee, her father, Lloyd Maines, had sent Martie and Emily a copy of a demo tape Natalie made at Berklee. Clearly, he was beginning to think his daughter might have a future in music.

Apparently, so did Martie and Emily, for they went to Lubbock and asked Natalie to record the vocal for their new song. When they returned with the demo tape, according to drummer Tom Van Schaik, they told everyone they had asked Natalie to sing the song because Laura was visiting her daughter in El Paso and was not available.

As the drama over Natalie's substituting for Laura on the demo tape unfolded, the group continued with a busy touring schedule. By the end of the summer, they had made their second appearance on *CBS This Morning* to sing "Oh, What a Beautiful Morning"; shared the stage with Patsy Montana at the Hope, Arkansas, Watermelon Festival; survived an Internal Revenue Service audit; gone white-water rafting before taking the stage at a concert at State Bridge, Colorado; and watched

Emily blow out twenty-three candles on an oversized chocolate banjo prepared for her birthday celebration.

Katie Pruett, an on-air personality at KYNG in Dallas, says the Dixie Chicks were frequent visitors to the radio station during the mid-1990s. "It was hard to live in Dallas and not know about the Dixie Chicks," Pruett told the author. "They've been up here a few times trying to get records played, and they were always singing the national anthem somewhere.

"One day—and it was really sweet of them to do it—they brought up the prettiest pair of balloon earrings made out of some cool metal, like titanium. I wore them for forever."

Pruett said she was not surprised to learn that the Chicks finally obtained a recording contract, but "I never thought that not getting a contract was an issue of talent, but rather of God. We get records here at the station from people, and I don't know how they get contracts because I hear local bands who are much better."

On September 12, 1995, *Good Morning Texas,* an early morning Dallas television show, celebrated its first anniversary with a special program that featured the Dixie Chicks, Texas Governor George W. Bush, and Dallas Cowboys running back Emmitt Smith. With the Chicks was their new guitarist Tommy Nash, who had recently joined the band.

In fashionable dress, the group performed live, with Martie on mandolin and Emily on acoustic guitar. After the performance, cohost Deborah Duncan told the viewing audience that the band had flown into Dallas at five o'clock that morning to be on the program.

"The last time you were on the show was . . . ?" said cohost Scott Sams, pausing to draw the women into conversation.

"We were here talking about the Fort Worth–Dallas Ballet," said Laura.

Sams later asked them about their trip to Europe.

"Six weeks ago we went to Belgium, and we headlined a big country festival over there," Laura said. "They think we're really famous over there. They bought every T-shirt and CD we brought. And we're headed to Austin at the end of this month to do a big fund-raiser for Lady Bird Johnson at her Wildflower Research Center. She's really gracious, and it's really going to be a great event."

"You did the Minnesota state fair, didn't you?" said Sams. "How was it?"

"It was great," said Laura. "We have turned into funnel cakes."

"And corn dogs," laughed Emily.

Sams asked about their new guitarist.

"Tommy Nash," said Laura. "We're so proud of him. He's been on the road with Ray Price, Moe Bandy, and Janie Fricke. And he's even played *Hee Haw*. We're just thrilled to have him." As Laura was talking about him, the camera zoomed in for a close-up of Nash, and he mouthed, "Hi Mom."

"Ya'll are Dixie Chicks," said Duncan. "Is he a Dixie rooster?"

"I guess so," said Emily.

"He's the fox in the hen house," added Laura.

Later in the show, the Dixie Chicks joined the staff of *Good Morning Dallas*, with everyone gathered around a large anniversary cake, and sang "Happy Anniversary" to the show staffers at the ABC affiliate.

Throughout the program, Emily seemed noticeably uncomfortable relating to Laura. There had never been any bad blood between Laura and Martie, but over the years it was Laura and Emily who had formed an especially close bond.

You could see it on the stage when something funny happened, for it would be Laura and Emily who automatically glanced at one another. And when Emily was doing a solo on the dobro, Laura's eyes beamed with admiration.

By the time the women appeared on *Good Morning Dallas*, major changes were underway within the group, but they were changes known only to Martie and Emily. Perhaps Natalie Maines' college wildlife course was not so much marking time as it was preparation for a possible appearance at Lady Bird Johnson's Wildflower Research Center.

The Dixie Chicks were right to showcase their new guitarist, Tommy Nash. He was a seasoned professional in his forties who, as Laura pointed out on *Good Morning Dallas*, had toured with some of country music's heavyweights. Musically, he was rock solid.

Nash's wife, Vicki, recalls the day the Chicks called to talk to him about joining the band. "I took the phone call, actually—it was in the early evening," Vicki remembers. "This voice said, 'I'm Laura with the Dixie Chicks, and we'd like to talk to Tommy about playing with us.'"

Vicki cupped her hand over the mouthpiece of the phone and spoke to her husband, who was lying in bed next to her. "I said, 'Dixie

Chicks—that sounds like a bunch of old women.' I asked him if he had ever heard of them, and he said he had. He got on the phone and they asked him to meet them at Emily's house the next day for an audition. They hired him on the spot."

Vicki said it was her understanding that Sony Records had given the girls Tommy's name.

When Tommy came home and told her that he had accepted a job playing with the Dixie Chicks, she couldn't wait to see the band in person. Any band named the Dixie Chicks would be worth seeing.

"With a name like Dixie Chicks, I didn't know what to expect," she says. "I thought, 'Oh, my God, they'll all be playing banjos.' But I was impressed. I took my daughter, who is now twenty-eight, to the concert with me. The girls were beautiful and I thought, 'Oh, wow!' They weren't anything like what I expected."

In the beginning, Vicki and her friends went to the Chicks' concerts often. "When he first started playing with them, they did a lot of local stuff," she explains. "I went all the time, and it was like family. Once they signed with Sony, they were gone all the time, so I viewed it with mixed emotions."

Vicki and Tommy have been married for thirty years and have five children, now ranging in age from fifteen to thirty. "It's great that they are doing so well," Vicki said, "but it's been lonely for a wife."

Despite all the troubles associated with recording an album, the Dixie Chicks pressed on, hopeful that if they stayed on course, everything would work out the way they wanted it to. Their next big booking was with a company named Corporate Magic, a talent agency that supplied major corporate clients with entertainers for their conventions and sales presentations.

The group had done other bookings with Corporate Magic. Once they had accepted a six-week booking for the company, which had put them up in plush, private rooms in San Francisco and Palm Beach, Florida, while performing in those cities.

"It was fabulous," Laura says. "In Palm Beach, we stayed at the Royal Brazilian Court and played there for two weeks with Liza Minnelli. Bob Newhart was the host, and Larry King was like a guest master of ceremonies for the show. They had hired us for another event, and it was going to take place in November 1995 and run for twelve to eighteen days. It was a big contract, over one hundred thousand dollars. We had reservations at a nice hotel. We were just expected to go to the venue, perform, and then back to our rooms. It wasn't like the [usual] road life."

Early on the morning of October 30, 1995, before nine A.M., Laura received a telephone call from Martie and Emily. They asked if they could stop by her house to chat. Laura thought it probably had something to do with the upcoming Corporate Magic booking.

"I was re-doing my house on Purdue Street [in Dallas], which was built in the 1930s," recalls Laura. "I was getting rid of some things just as Emily was putting her house together on Van Ness. When I wasn't going to use a rug anymore, before I offered it to Goodwill or a neighbor, I would call Emily and ask if she needed it. She'd say, yes or no, or what color is it? I gave her an old radio and some other stuff."

Only a few days before the October 30 meeting, Laura had given Emily some of her household furnishings. In retrospect she thinks those generous gestures played a role in the timing of the visit. Emily has a heart as big as a Texas moon, and it is not in her nature to accept gifts under what could later be construed as false pretenses.

So there they were on October 30, the Dixie Chicks engaged in a powwow at a little after nine in the morning. The fact that Martie and Emily wanted to come over to her house at that time of the day was disconcerting enough, for neither sister has a reputation as an early bird, but when Laura saw the determined look in their eyes, she knew trouble was afoot.

"We want to make a change," one of the siblings said. "We need to get with the market and do something different musically."

Martie and Emily told Laura they wanted to buy her out of the band, effective that day.

"Do you have a replacement in mind?" Laura asked, stunned.

"Yeah, Natalie Maines," they answered. "She's been working up the material."

"But what about the contracts?" Laura asked. "What about the Corporate Magic contract?"

"We're gonna go meet with Corporate Magic and audition Natalie with them, and go forward from there."

"They are so timid usually, I knew there was no changing it," says Laura. "I just said, I want just one thing—never say I quit, even if it is the easy thing to do."

The only remaining question was the terms of the split-up. In true

Dixie Chick fashion, the women gathered together in a circle with notepads on their laps. They agreed that each woman would write down what she thought would be a fair buyout price. Then, on signal, they held up the notepads for all to see.

"It was almost the same thing," recalls Laura. "It was amazing how close to the same number we all came. We just worded it differently. All along we knew we thought alike—and in the end we did."

When Martie and Emily left the house that day, Laura was devastated. For six years, she had devoted her life to the Dixie Chicks. Now they were no longer a part of her life. It had ended in a blink of an eye.

"I put a lot of things on hold, willingly, because the band was my first priority. Marketing that band was the only thing I thought of when I woke up in the morning. I was always thinking about how I could market the band. I would never have quit. I loved that band. I love that band today. I cried so hard I thought I would never smile again. That sounds so melodramatic, especially when I compare it to how much I love my child, but I loved the band so much. It was so important to my life."

The first thing Laura did after they left was to get on the telephone. She called one of her sisters. Her best friend, Catherine. A couple of other friends. "I scanned my memory for anything and everything that I could have ever said that would have hurt Martie and Emily's feelings. Ever. I could only come up with two incidents that went haywire between us, but we had moved past them completely in two days' time, and those had happened years ago . . . I began to hate myself. I prayed about my flawed personality, non-existent waistline and crow's-feet.

"I was from a slightly different generation than Martie and Emily. I was in college in the mid-1970s while they were in first grade, so naturally I had a large collection of disco albums that I boogied to and warmed up my voice before shows. I went to my collection and realized how corny and dated I was.

"You know how when you get hurt or you're in a real hard place you go to the Voice. The Voice that makes it better? The Voice of maybe your youth or your home place or a grandmother comes to you and you can hear it and you know if you listen you'll be OK? Well, I have that voice, and it comes from my home place at the Guadalupe Mountains in west Texas . . .

"When everything goes haywire, and the shit really hits the fan, I can be found at Rosita's Café in Dell City with a chili relleno in my mouth and [longtime friend] Norma Stringer by my side with her Silver Belly Stetson on her head. She wears it only for special or dire situations. So, I went there, first in my mind, then via Southwest Airlines three days later, and I stayed in my own bed at Daddy's house at the ranch and I bawled."

At the time, Laura was shocked by the incident. However, as she thought about it over the coming months, she saw things that had seemed insignificant at the time but important in retrospect.

"I think Emily and Martie were talking about it for months," says Laura. "Early in the summer, we played Lovett [Texas] and Natalie [Maines] came out and had a notebook at the show. I didn't think anything about it. It was Lloyd's little girl. She didn't seem all that interested in the music, but she did get the board tapes [of the songs performed] that night."

Right after Martie and Emily left Laura's house that day, two of the members of the band, guitarist Tommy Nash and bassist Bobby Benjamin, appeared on Laura's front porch. "Is it true?" they asked.

Lynch assured them that it was indeed true.

"Oh, my god," they said to Laura. "If it could happen to you, what about us?"

As the band members were headed to Laura's porch, Emily and Martie went to pick up Natalie, as Laura later learned, who was waiting for them at Emily's house. They took her directly over to the office of Corporate Magic so the executives there could meet her. They auditioned her there on the spot and received a thumbs-up for Natalie to carry out Laura's part of the contract.

Not making an appearance on Laura's porch was drummer Tom Van Schaik, who had been tipped off about the coup the day before. "The sisters took me aside and said this is what is going down Monday," he divulges. "I said, 'What!' It was totally out of left field. I had no idea there was any thought of changes. They said, 'Monday we will offer to buy Laura out, and Natalie will be the new singer.' They wanted to know where I stood. From what I gathered, they had their management behind the move. I don't think they would have done it without having the manager behind it fully."

Of all the people who had been associated with the Chicks over the years, it was probably Van Schaik who had the most respect for Laura's voice and for her business and ethical sense. Research for this book revealed no individual who did not profess admiration for Laura and her talent, and, certainly, Van Schaik was at the top of that list. A job is a job is a job, but playing with the Chicks had always been more than that to him.

At first, Van Schaik wasn't sure if Laura was opposed to the idea. "She didn't seem as happy out on the road," he says. "I just figured she was beginning to fray around the edges. I thought maybe she was tired of Nashville saying her voice was not commercial enough. I loved Laura like a sister, and I hated to see her leave.

"Natalie's voice is exactly what Nashville was looking for. Natalie has a powerhouse voice. She'll blow the back doors off the building. It was sad to see Laura go, but looking back I can see that the sisters thought, 'This is our shot to get to that star status.'"

It's now several years since her "surprise retirement party"—a phrase Laura coined to describe her exit from the band—but she remains to this day one of the Dixie Chicks' biggest fans. She cringes when she thinks about how difficult it must have been for the sisters to ask her to leave the band.

"I had never seen them so exact," Laura remembers. "I had seen them a lot of ways, but never that way. It was horrible. I'm such a strong personality, imagine the feelings they had looking at each other, saying, 'OK, now we're in front of her house, and now we've got to go inside and do it.'" Laura can laugh about it now. "It did take two of them," she says, laughing. "It must have been scary for them."

The night after Laura's "surprise retirement party," was October 31. "I went to a friend's house for Halloween," she says. "It was him, his wife, their children, and their neighbors. We had this big, huge cauldron full of Halloween candy, and I remember watching all these Tinker Bells and pirates come down the street to trick-or-treat—and I couldn't stop crying. I bawled my head off. I didn't tell my mother anything, because she would have cried more than I did."

Somewhere in the Fort Worth–Dallas area are trick-or-treaters who can remember being greeted by a Dixie Chick clutching a cauldron of candy soaked with the tears of dashed dreams.

DIVA CHICK DIGS CLAWS INTO SHAKY ROOST

1996–1997

Almost overnight, Natalie Maines, who never particularly cared for country music, was anointed Diva Chick. Natalie was reputedly given a one-third ownership of the Dixie Chicks, simply for signing on the dotted line.

Rumors persist that Sony purchased the Chicks' merchandising rights from the women for a small amount, but the Japanese-owned record label steadfastly refuses to discuss any aspect of their contractual arrangement with the band. When asked point-blank to confirm or deny a merchandising agreement, a Sony executive refused to discuss it. "Let's not go there," snapped the woman, who subsequently left Sony to pursue other interests.

As time went by, it became increasingly apparent that Laura's "retirement" was dictated by the record label and the Chicks' management, that it did not originate with Martie and Emily. According to *Rolling Stone* magazine, management informed the sisters that Laura was out in favor of a new singer, a "firecracker." Says coproducer Blake Chancey about the addition of Natalie, "When they kicked off the first song, it was just this upbeat, turbo-rocking song. It was unbelievable. And then Natalie opened her mouth, and I went, 'Oh, we've got something here.'"

Rolling Stone speculates that Chancey was simply turned off by Laura's "soft-folk" sound, but there was probably more to it than that. At thirty-six, Laura was well beyond the age considered optimum for new female artists. Then there was her dark-eyed, dark-haired appearance, a product of her Irish-Hispanic heritage. So-called "ethnic artists" have thrived on the pop charts—witness the success of Sony's own Mariah Carey or Gloria Estefan—but the reality of the country music business is that you can probably count on one hand all the new artists signed over the past thirty years who were over thirty-five or ethnic in appearance. For a time, Laura considered talking to a lawyer about a discrimination lawsuit—she would have had two salient counts on which to base one—but she never pursued it, primarily because of her strong affection for the sisters.

Within two weeks of the Halloween "massacre," Natalie went on the road with the girls. "With Natalie, that's when the wheels started rolling around," says Martie in the Sony official bio. "You could tell there was excitement. There was energy."

"Martie and Emily had always been the best part of the Dixie Chicks," says Natalie. "I had been waiting for my shot."

The only problem was that while Natalie had the voice, she wasn't overly poised, and no one knew if she possessed that special girl-glue chemistry that seems be a factor in holding all-girl groups together.

"We had less than two weeks to get ready after the change," drummer Tom Van Schaik reports. "It was a lot of rehearsal and getting Natalie used to playing the songs. She brought in a couple of blues tunes she had been singing. Most of it was on Natalie's shoulders to remember all the songs and the words.

"The first couple of shows were kind of nerve-wracking, but I don't think there were any major train wrecks. Everyone was so focused on getting the band tight. There wasn't any real time to hang and get to know each other. There were no major personality clashes. She fit right in."

Looking back on it, Martie confided to *Country Weekly,* finding Natalie was the "best thing that ever happened to Emily and me."

For Van Schaik, the oddest part of it all was audience reaction. "The initial reactions were of shock because everyone expected the two sisters and Laura. All of a sudden there's Natalie. I had to answer dozens of questions after every show. There wasn't any throwing of vegetables, but it was clear that it was a totally different voice that was leading the band." Fan reaction to the change ranged from surprise to, "Oh, that's show business for you."

"Natalie is a much stronger lead singer, but the ironic thing is that it was Laura who held them together year after year," says former manager David Skepner. "When one [of the sisters] wanted to go to the Air Force Academy and another one wanted to do something else, Laura was the one who held it together. Then a stronger lead singer came in [and they asked her to leave]."

As Natalie was learning the ropes as a Chick, Laura sobbed almost continuously. Every time the tears subsided, something new would come up and start them flowing again. Two months after she was asked to leave the Chicks, the group was booked at a performance at Billy Bob's in Fort Worth. It marked the first time Natalie sang with the group in its old stomping grounds.

Laura's sister, Christina, asked her if she wanted to go to the concert.

"I thought, 'I'll be all right. I just gotta see what is so much better about this new situation,'" Laura relates. "As I sat there in Billy Bob's, I thought I could keep my composure, but tears just rolled from my face. Of course, I was most conspicuous because everyone there knew me . . . They were saying, 'There's this new girl and she doesn't sound that good, and here's Laura sitting at a table.' It was a bummer of a thing. I wish I had not gone. It was bad judgment to go, but I was just too curious."

Laura's eyes brighten as she conveys the experience, her outstretched hands showing her frustration. "That's a girl thing," she says with a smile. "Gotta go see! Gotta know! Gotta have our face right in it! The pain is not bad enough just knowing from hearsay. We gotta go put our face in it."

During the concert, Laura tried to make eye contact with her old friend, Lloyd Maines, who performed with the band that night, but he would not look at her. She spotted a new face moving on and off the stage, a longhaired guy who seemed to know who she was. It was Michael Tarabay, Natalie's boyfriend.

Later in the show, Michael approached Laura and introduced himself. He had been driving the van for the girls for the past several weeks (since Laura's departure) and somehow felt like Laura was sort of family.

"He walked up to me and said, 'Hi, I'm Natalie's boyfriend,'" Laura recalls. "I said, 'Oh, it's a bad night to meet me.' He seemed nice enough, though."

Laura left the concert that night determined to get on with the rest of her life. Her biggest unanswered question was, what does a thirty-seven-year-old former Dixie Chick do next? Unlike former Chick Robin

Macy, who had left several years earlier, she had absolutely no desire to start up another band. (Robin was still performing in 1995, but her visibility in the music business was rapidly declining.) No one who has never played in a band could ever understand the energy, pain, and disappointment of it all. Most people who have been burned never go back for seconds.

After she got all the crying out of her system, the next thing Laura did was to call an old friend, Roy Bode. The former editor of the *Dallas Times-Herald* from 1988 until it went out of business in 1991, Bode had since taken a public relations position with the University of Texas Southwestern Medical Center. They had first met when the Dixie Chicks performed for the U.S. Marshals Posse, a mounted equestrian group that helped charities raise money for special projects.

"I'm not a music expert," Bode observes, "but they played the kind of music I like, and they seemed to be one of the most sought after country groups around."

When Bode learned Laura was in need of a job, he offered her a position as his assistant at the University of Texas. "She was unhappy about it [being asked to leave the band]," he says. "She was at kind of a loss as to where to go and what to do. She was trying to figure out what her next move was. She was fairly sure she was not going to stay in music. She was ready to get out of the music industry. She was hurt by what was really her eviction by the band. I don't know if they're saying they didn't throw her out, but they threw her out, no doubt about it."

Today, Bode still follows the group, though he says he doesn't think Dallas feels as connected to them as they did before. "I think they've got a different type of music than they had," he says. "In the past, they did more western swing, although they recorded some classic tunes. But today it is definitely a Nashville sound. They are doing a good job doing what they are doing."

It was while she was working for Bode that Laura encountered a family friend named Mac Tull. When Laura was about sixteen, Tull had dated her older sister. Laura barely noticed him at the time; she was then more interested in non-dating pursuits.

When they reestablished social contact twenty years later, Tull asked, "What's new?" and Laura answered that she was no longer with the Chicks. When she inquired of him, "So what's new with you?" Tull said he had married and divorced and had just won thirty million dollars in the Texas lottery.

Actually, they were a perfect match. Tull is a tall, soft-spoken cowboy whose low-keyed personality seems a perfect match for Laura Lynch's more mercurial temperament. After dating for more than a year and a half, Laura and Mac were married.

"Mac filled this place that had been inside me for a long time," Laura says. "I hadn't had true love since I was a young girl. It made all the difference in the world."

Today, Tull is a successful rancher who owns a nice spread a short distance outside Fort Worth. With its Spanish-style courthouse and town square, the nearest town looks like something straight out of a spaghetti western (with the exception of the Cadillacs and BMWs parked on the square, of course).

Laura and Mac's ranch is located on miles of green pasture land and seems like an oasis of tranquillity. The house is spacious and rambling, filled with photographs and artwork.

Upstairs in the loft is Laura's "Chick" room. It is where she keeps years of memorabilia, photographs, T-shirts, demo tapes, and just about anything you can think of that could ever have been associated with the Chicks.

Looking through the trunks and big boxes, she becomes childlike as she displays a new treasure to a visitor, her eyes beaming as the object brings back loving memories of her association with the band. A closet contains dozens of Dixie Chicks costumes. They are as bright as sunlight and seem dazzling just hanging on the rods in the closet.

Laura goes through the costumes like a shopper at a rummage sale, holding up first one, then another, for examination. One costume is so loaded with rhinestones and bits of glitter that it must weigh twenty pounds.

"Oh, well," Laura says, finally closing the door. "It's the way it was."

"I saw the Dixie Chicks being interviewed a long time before *Wide Open Spaces,* and Natalie was talking, and I thought to myself, 'She's got a radio voice, and if she doesn't make it in the music business, she should do radio,'" says Leigh Browning, director of broadcasting at West Texas A&M. "She has had some vocal training, or she is very deliberate when she speaks. Anytime I hear anything like that, it gets my attention."

One of the first places the Dixie Chicks performed after Natalie joined the group was at South Plains College in Levelland. Not only was Natalie a former student, but Papa Maines served on an advisory committee to the school and occasionally taught courses. The Dixie Chicks performed for the school's Cancer Society Ball.

The thought was in the right place, but it was probably not the best type of venue for Natalie to display her vocal skills. "They were not really a dance band, which was what the audience was used to, so people said they couldn't dance to their music," says Stephen John, director of college relations at South Plains College. "They were well received, though."

Falling into the category of precursors of things to come, the Chicks performed at Billy Bob's in Dallas—this is the same night Laura attended and sobbed her heart out—and since Papa Maines had performed there the night before with Jerry Jeff Walker, the Chicks had asked him to stay over and play with them for their show.

What happened next, says Cary Banks, was vintage Natalie Maines: They were all set up and ready to go when Natalie approached her father. Banks chuckles when he thinks about what came next. "Natalie is all of five-foot-nothing, and her dad is six-foot-three and weighs two hundred and forty pounds. So she gets right in his face and says, 'Old man, remember, tonight you're working for me.'"

Banks wasn't being critical of Natalie. It's just that he thinks of her as a rambunctious pup that grew up to become a star. If she's got the nerve to sass the Godfather of Texas Music, then power to her.

Banks still can't believe that it's little Natalie who's getting all those people in the audience so worked up. Says Banks: "She and Lloyd have the same personality. They are very strong-willed people. She's an extremely opinionated person."

During all of the early adjustments, Martie and Emily assumed the role of tour guide and translator for Natalie. One of the first places the sisters took Natalie was Jay Rury's Violin Shop.

"Martie and Natalie came in, and Martie introduced Natalie to us," recalls Rury. "Martie said that Sony wanted them to change their style, to more of a Mary Chapin Carpenter kind of image. They did that, then went on to the generation-x style they have now."

There was a lot of talk around Dallas about Laura leaving, Rury says. "The Chicks were real secretive about it. No one knows what the real story was. It was like, 'Laura's out, Natalie's in—' Boom!"

Despite all the talk on the street, the Texas media was slow to catch up with the story. One of the most negative accounts to come out, according to Laura, appeared in the *Fort Worth Weekly,* a freebie publication. The night before the newspaper hit the stands, Emily and Martie called Laura and told her about the feature story.

They had done the interview willingly because they thought it would be a positive mirror of the women's relationships with each other, but when they saw an advance copy of the article they were horrified. They told Laura the tone of the article was negative, and they hoped she didn't blame them.

"How bad can it be?" Laura asked.

"It's bad," they said. "They tricked us. They said they were going to do one angle, and they did another."

"It was a terrible, terrible article," insists Laura, who rushed out the morning after the telephone call to pick up one of the free newspapers that were distributed all over town. The Dixie Chicks were the cover story for the weekly issue. When she saw the photograph, she liked it. She thought it was cute. Then when she read the article, she was horrified, for she felt it was mean-spirited, backstabbing—everything the Dixie Chicks were not.

When Laura's daughter, Asia, read the article, she started crying: "How can they write this?"

"It's OK, honey. I just wanted you to see. Now we gotta get busy."

With Asia at the wheel of Laura's Tahoe truck, they went from newsstand to newsstand throughout the city. The sign on the newsstand said "free," so the disenfranchised Chick helped herself.

"If they think those issues flew off the stand, they are absolutely right," Laura says. "They flew off the stands a hundred at a time into the back of my Tahoe with my child at the wheel. We went to the dumpsite and pitched them. When we were done, I was heaving, and my daughter looked so cute. She's such a team player. I wondered if their advertisers thought they got good coverage that week?"

When asked about the Great Newspaper Caper, Asia gasps. "My heart was beating," she says. "It was hilarious. We were in downtown Fort Worth, and I'm sure all the people around were looking and saying, 'I wonder what that is all about?'"

Actually, in her horror, Laura may have done the *Fort Worth Weekly* a big favor. The newspaper had only been in operation for a short time, and Laura's unexpected circulation "boost" allowed them to post some pretty terrific circulation numbers—at least on paper.

*   *   *

By the spring of 1996, Dixie Chicks drummer Tom Van Schaik began to notice not-so-subtle changes in the operation of the band. "In the very beginning, practically three-fourths of the way through my tenure with the group, they openly discussed music things and asked for our input," he says. "There was a big change when they signed with Simon [Renshaw] at Senior Management. All of a sudden there was no more discussion about anything going on businesswise. It was almost like that area of communication was cut off."

Van Schaik never warmed up to Renshaw, probably because the manager was not shy about letting band members know they were disposable. "Personally, I did not really trust him a lot," says Van Schaik. "Once, in front of the guys, he said sidemen were a dime a dozen in Nashville. I had been with the Chicks for four and a half years at that point. I thought, 'Wait a minute, I've got a lot invested in this thing.'"

In May 1996, the Dixie Chicks went to Japan, where American executives for the Japanese-owned record label introduced the women to the holders of their recording contract. Before the band left for Japan, the mayor of Dallas presented the women with a basket of Texas products and gifts to give to the Japanese.

Although most of their appearances in Japan were scheduled on American military bases, they did perform one show in a 2,500-seat venue in Kumamoto, as part of a country music festival.

"There was lots of press at the theatre," recalls Van Schaik. "They asked us to do a meet-and-greet in the lobby. All these Japanese came in wearing cowboy garb—with chaps, holsters, and guns. It was pretty funny." Van Schaik doesn't recall any questions arising about the band's name. They just accepted it as a band name. Says Van Schaik: "Pretty girls playing well just blew their minds."

The trip went smoothly, says Van Schaik, except for a few unnerving occasions when the Chicks decided to go to the officers' or enlisted men's clubs. You can practically hear the sweat in Van Schaik's voice when he says, "We had to make sure there were always guys on both sides of the girls."

As if all the musical changes were not enough, Natalie's personal life changed drastically on May 9, 1997, when she married Michael Tarabay, her boyfriend from South Plains College. Natalie was twenty-three and Michael was twenty-seven.

They moved into a Warfield Drive house in Nashville to set up housekeeping, and Michael, a bassist, offered his services as a driver, roadie, whatever, to the Dixie Chicks.

With each change in the group, there seemed to be a ripple effect. That summer, drummer Tom Van Schaik decided he had had enough behind-the-scenes Chickadee intrigue. Talk about the recording project was coming and going at record speed, but the more he heard about the songs—and the more he was being cut out of the decision-making process—the more he realized he had reached the end of the road with the Dixie Chicks.

As a result, Van Schaik resigned and took a job as the drummer with the Robert Earl Keen band. It was painful leaving the group, because traveling with the Chicks was as much a crusade for him as it was employment. You had to be a true believer just to be able to hold on over the rough spots.

Van Schaik remembers when believing was hard on all of them. What kept him going was hearing the women talk about the Dream. "The talk on the van was always about having a major label behind them," he reveals. "Just to get that country stardom! Laura wanted that Tammy Wynette sort of fame, that stardom. That was always the talk. Then there was the frustration of the rejection of Nashville, them not knowing what to do with the girls. The girls kept saying, 'Look, we're selling records.'"

"I respect [Renshaw] for the success he's had with the girls, but working with Robert Earl Keen, his approach is just the opposite," Van Schaik said in an interview just prior to Easter 1999. "Keen takes care of everyone working for him. He's always trying to get us endorsements and things like that. He's flying everyone [in the band] home for Easter. Our last date out this tour is the day before Easter. He's buying everyone air tickets home so they can be with their family on Easter."

As Martie, Emily, and Natalie struggled to finish their first album together, they were tossed around like cabbages in the back of a flatbed truck.

Most Nashville studios prefer that recording artists work with seasoned session players. The reasoning behind that is that recording is a unique mixture of art and science, and the place for the regular band to learn the music is out on the road and not in the studio. It's also why some concertgoers leave the fairground saying, "That don't sound exactly like it did on the record!"

The Dixie Chicks were not unique; their band members were pretty much squeezed out of the picture, except for Tommy Nash who did the arrangements. What was unusual was the way the production chores kept changing. Paul Worley was added as a second producer to assist artists and repertoire executive Blake Chancey.

As the months went by, other producers were added for individual songs. Legendary producer Billy Sherrill, who produced Tammy Wynette's biggest hits, was hired to work on one song ("Give It Up Or Let Me Go"). Eric Legg was hired for the other songs and given two assistants to get the job done.

Fifteen musicians are credited with playing on *Wide Open Spaces,* including Papa Lloyd Maines, Greg Morrow (a much-in-demand drummer from Memphis who is probably best known for his work with Amy Grant), guitarist Billy Joe Walker Jr., and guitarist Mark Casstevens.

Exactly how many songs, musicians, and producers they went through before they completed the album is a closely guarded secret. But when all the worry, sweat, agony, and uncertainty was over, the Dixie Chicks ended up with twelve songs.

"You Were Mine," the song Martie and Emily cowrote and asked Natalie to sing before Laura left the group, was the only song on the album written by the Dixie Chicks. It is laced with Papa Maines's steel guitar licks, a gesture that keeps it solidly in the country fold. But it is the sweet harmony and Martie's loving fiddle parts, oddly enough, that transport the song out of traditional country and into the honky-tonk fantasies of generation-x.

"I was surprised at how it sounded," Natalie told the *Los Angeles Times,* referring to the time she sang on the original demo. "I figured that if they wrote that, then that's where they wanted to go with the music. I could go there, I told them. I couldn't be the bluegrass cowgirl singer. But I could sing 'You Were Mine.'"

When they began the album, "You Were Mine" was the only song they knew for certain they wanted to include. In keeping with her alternative and blues interests, Natalie brought in several numbers, including Bonnie Raitt's "Give It Up Or Let Me Go," on which Emily and Martie alternated solos that are as hypnotic in their energy as in their precision.

"Give It Up Or Let Me Go" was produced by Billy Sherrill, who broke new ground in the 1970s and 1980s with Tammy Wynette, George

Jones, David Allen Coe, and others. Some consider him one of the best producers of female talent who ever walked Nashville's Music Row.

"Wide Open Spaces," a song by Susan Gibson, an emerging recording artist and fellow Texan, is a fairly traditional song musically. However, the lyrics seem to have been mined from the deep recesses of Gibson's seemingly disaffected youth, and they speak to the need for making that first reach for freedom.

"Let 'er Rip" is an up-tempo, rockabilly tune, complete with rippling piano keys, that allows Natalie to rub her gritty voice up against the pounding rhythm of the guitars and piano. "Am I the Only One (Who's Ever Felt This Way)" by Maria McKee was previously recorded by Lone Justice, a country group popular in the 1980s.

Once the album was completed and titled, no one was quite sure what they had. On the negative side, they had only one song written by band members (songwriting ability is often an indicator of longevity in the country music industry), and the song selection didn't seem to follow any recognizable theme. On the positive side, they had included a lot of cover tunes, songs that had done reasonably well in previous incarnations.

The biggest plus was the women themselves. They had SPUNK, and if Martie and Emily could not charm an audience with their feminine ways, Natalie seemed prepared to kick their citified butts from one row to the next to get their attention. If anyone in country music has ever been hungrier for success, no one has yet found them.

Once the album was finished, it resembled nothing so much as it did a patchwork quilt. Music executives didn't know whether they had a hit or a huge embarrassment. In the backs of their minds all this time had been the realization that every record label in Nashville had passed on the Dixie Chicks at one time or another.

Oddly enough, as work on the album seesawed back and forth, Laura received an unexpected honor. *Bass Player* magazine has a regular feature entitled "Unsung Bass Stylists" in which it salutes bassists it feels have been overlooked. For its April 1997 issue, it chose to honor Laura Lynch for her work on the 1992 album, *Little Ol' Cowgirl*. Said the magazine: "Her warm tone, unusual note choices, and subtle fills keep things interesting—but most of all, she has great phrasing. Her work adds an unobtrusive but vital sophistication to this eclectic, adventurous record . . ."

CHICKS DRAG DREAM INTO WIDE OPEN SPACES

1998

On February 4, 1998, less than a week after the release of the first single, "I Can Love You Better," Monument Records issued a press release under this double headline: "Dixie Chicks Make Dazzling Debut / Texas Trio Are Highest Debuting Group in Seven Years." *Wide Open Spaces* was listed as Number 17 on the *Billboard* album charts.

"Dixie Chicks are easily one of the most exciting new acts to emerge in a long time," said Mike Kraski, senior vice president of sales and marketing at the record label, in one of the first press releases issued on the group. "Not only are they first rate musicians, they are also world-class singers and songwriters. We were floored the first time we saw them perform and knew they were the perfect flagship act for the newly resurrected Monument Records."

In the video for "I Can Love You Better," the women seemed surprisingly ill at ease and uncomfortable. Except for the promotional video made several years earlier by their manager, which was composed mostly of clips from television shows, it was the first video that featured the group performing an individual song. The saving grace of the video was Natalie's brief, hyperactive interactions with the camera, where she rushed at the lens and made spastic motions with her hands. Martie and Emily seemed highly amused by her antics.

Reviews of the album itself, the group's fourth, were mixed:

Longtime fans of this Texas trio will be thrilled . . . (they) have a fresh, earthy sound buoyed by Maines' distinctive vocal. The song has a catchy chorus, but otherwise it's just a rather cliched, assembly-line lyric.—*Billboard*

The Dixie Chicks are shaping up to be the first breakout country act of 1998.—*USA Today*

This is an old-fashioned, good-time album, affable and rich with sweet-tone melodies.—*People*

Taking a more critical view of the disc was the Texas media. In the *Austin Chronicle* Christopher Hess wrote: "The music is bland, the lyrics recount predictable scripts that have been written into pop songs for as long as they've existed, and about the only way to tell this is supposed to be country as opposed to pop are the strings—and Papa Maines on steel guitar."

Writing in the *Dallas Observer*, Robert Wilonsky noted that the Dixie Chicks had come a long way since the days the band paid for the release of its own albums: "No band in town ever worked harder to get further; outsiders will write of their overnight success, but the Chicks know better. So do Robin Macy and Laura Lynch, women who defined the band's sound from the beginning only to find themselves barely even mentioned in the band's Monument biography, referred to only as 'two other original members.' Macy and Lynch were sacrifices made on the altar of country-music success."

Wilonsky bemoaned the absence of the group's frilly dresses and retro-cowgirl image and noted that those things had been replaced by images with which country radio is more familiar. The reviewer wrote: "The Dixie Chicks are now Nashville women, not so different from the other produce Music City produces and reduces every day."

As the album continued to climb the charts, executives at the record label were amazed. "Dixie Chicks are a perfect example of how great music shines through," said a label executive in yet another press release that pointed out that the girls had made appearances on CNN, *The View*, and the *Sally Jessy Raphael Show*.

Hard-core Texas fans, the ones who stuck with the girls over the years, were pleased with the group's sudden burst of success, but not so certain they had not lost something in the process. Says music store owner Jay Rury: "I don't think their sound now is as good as the old sound, where all four of them were part of the sound. Now it's just mostly Natalie Maines up front with the lead. You don't hear the instruments like you used to. Emily is probably the most talented on the instruments of the three of them, but you hardly hear her work, it's in the background. Natalie is in the front and the girls come in for some harmony. Of course, they've got professional players in the background. It sounds slick and canned."

Dallas radio personality Katie Pruett says that KYNG was the first station in that city to play the girls' new single, "I Can Love You Better." Says Pruett: "They came up here [to the station] and did a lunch thing and sang the song live. It was really fun, and I thought, 'Gosh, I hope they do well,' but this is not a logical business."

Pruett says she has one hundred and fifty artist pages on her Web site (www.superstarcountry.com). "The Dixie Chicks are just huge here," she says. "They usually get fifteen hundred hits a month versus number two at one thousand hits. Until recently, Natalie [Maines] would be in Dallas for the weekend, and she would call to say hey. Now I don't imagine she even wants to look at a telephone when she is in Dallas. I would never want to be that famous."

During the spring of 1998, the Dixie Chicks continued to promote *Wide Open Spaces*. They could hardly believe the attention that the album was receiving. On the country charts they were beating out heavyweights such as Brooks and Dunn and Trisha Yearwood. On the pop charts, they were just slightly behind Pearl Jam and Everclear—and gaining fast.

The Chicks were used to dealing with enthusiastic fans, but the fame associated with a hit album seemed to draw fans from dark, new places. At a performance in New York, they were in their tour bus when a man started pounding on the closed door in a very menacing way. Obviously, he had made up his mind that he just had to get himself one of those Chicks.

Unknown to the man, also on board the bus were guitarist Tommy Nash, other members of the Chicks touring band, and Charlie Robison, a country singer Emily had befriended several months earlier at a concert near San Antonio. (Actually, they had been dating about two weeks but they had not yet started calling it that. Robison was a native Texan whose mother worked as a bartender at various honky-tonks around the state, most notably at a club named The Purple Cow.)

The man pounding on the door sent everyone into a panic. "Natalie was screaming for no one to get off the bus because he might have a gun," says Vicki Nash, the wife of Chicks guitarist Tommy Nash. "Everyone was lying down on the floor of the bus, and Natalie was calling 911 with her mobile phone. Meanwhile, this guy is tearing up the bus and calling out for these Texas boys to come outside to stop him."

Finally, the Texas boys had enough of that nonsense and decided to accommodate the man. They rushed off the bus and took the man down, leaving Robison to literally sit on him until the police arrived. Unfortunately, the police thought Robison was the troublemaker and quickly carted him off to jail.

"Emily was just boo-hooing, Tommy said, because Charlie was going off to jail," says Vicki. "Simon [Renshaw] was asleep in the hotel, and they woke him up to go get Charlie out of jail."

Robison spent several hours in jail before Renshaw could explain that Robison was the hero and not the villain. Says Vicki Nash: "When the police found out who they were, they asked for their autographs."

For Robison, it was just another unfortunate incident out on the road—Texas musicians are always getting into trouble for one reason or another; it's part of the job description—but for Emily it was exactly the sort of thing that Roy Rogers would have done for Dale Evans, and it got her attention in a way that roses or perfume never would have done. Robison was no cowboy, but he passed for one on that day, and Emily fell in love on the spot.

As the album continued to rise on the charts, record executives released the second single, "There's Your Trouble," in March 1998. To make the video, record executives turned to Thom Oliphant, one of the most creative videomakers working in Nashville. He was just wrapping up a project with B. B. King and Tracy Chapman when he got the assignment.

"I went to Houston to see them play at a University of Texas party that they had done for years and years," Oliphant remembers. "I didn't know that much about them, but they had an amazing energy I had not encountered that often. They showed a real desire to take chances. I was impressed by how fearless they really were. It's a charming trait, but a really rare trait."

Oliphant suggested they adopt a "South Asian honky-tonk" theme for "There's Your Trouble." Says Olpihant: "They didn't blink an eye. They said, 'Oh, that's a great idea.' They were so game."

The finished video resulted in a kaleidoscope of whirling images, bright red and blue colors, and fearless Chick attitude. The girls, all wearing dark slacks and shirts and jackets, performed on a runway that looked suspiciously like the ones strippers strut upon in Asian adult entertainment centers. Couples sat at tables around the runway.

Oliphant did a masterful job of merging the visual imagery of the Chicks with their music. It would become, in this critic's opinion, the single, most powerful ingredient of the group's success. Their music was good, but not strong enough to carry them to the top of the charts. Visuals were another matter.

Once the video was released, it quickly became apparent where the strongest fan base for the girls would lie: It would be with longtime fans of the women, and with teenage and preteen girls who latched onto the visual energy of the group. But being a fan of the Dixie Chicks was only part of it.

Like wildfire, word about the Dixie Chicks went out over the Internet. All over the United States and Canada fans, by the thousands, set up Web sites and communicated with each other. One of the first to set up a Web site was Robert Brooks of Dallas, a thirty-two-year-old computer programmer with American Airlines.

Brooks first heard the Dixie Chicks in 1991, when *A Prairie Home Companion* traveled to Dallas and had the Dixie Chicks as guests. A year later, the Chicks performed at an American Airlines picnic. "My wife and I both fell in love with their music and bought a tape that day, and we've been following them ever since," Brooks proclaims.

When the first single, "I Can Love You Better," was released in 1998, Brooks followed its progress closely with several radio stations and sent the Chicks e-mail letting them know how it was doing. From time to time, he received replies from the Chicks themselves thanking him for the information.

One of the Internet sites he especially enjoyed was called "Chick Chat." It was set up by the record label and allowed the Chicks to communicate directly with their fans. By mid-year 1998, however, they discontinued "Chick Chat," citing time constraints on the girls. Fans were urged to visit the record label's primary Web site used to publicize all of its recording artists.

Brooks was disappointed with that site because it ignored the long, colorful history of the Dixie Chicks, and he decided to create his own Internet site, one that would celebrate the band's rich Texas history.

Finding a name for the site was his first challenge. He searched the registry and found that "dixiechicks.com" had been registered but was no longer in use. He tracked down its owner and learned that it had originally been created for the Dixie Chicks management but had been dropped as a project. According to Brooks, the owner of the site was looking for someone who could put it to good use.

As a result, Brooks took over the Web site located at dixiechicks.com and began gathering photographs and early recordings to use as sound bytes. "I can't put as much time in it as I would like," he says. "I probably spend five to ten hours a week on it. The welcome page averages about one thousand hits a day."

Brooks was among the first to post pre-Natalie Maines information on his Web site. "The Dixie Chicks have a sound that is different than anything else coming out of Nashville," Brooks believes. "That sound has its roots in their long history . . . the disappointing part is that on the current album [*Wide Open Spaces*] you can't really hear the fiddle and the banjo like you could before. It's covered up by the generic studio musician sound, but it comes through some time. I'm hoping on their next album that the success of *Wide Open Spaces* will give them the ability to say, 'We want our instruments to come out more.'"

By March 1999, Brooks was asked to vacate dixiechicks.com. He established a new site at dixiechicks.mixedsignal.net. He says that, with only one day's notice and no explanation, ownership of dixiechicks.com was transferred to Simon Renshaw, the Dixie Chicks manager.

"Well, it was too good to last," Brooks regrets. "I wish the Dixie Chicks well and hope that their future Web site is as unique and successful as the Chicks themselves."

Brooks was unique among early Dixie Chicks Web site owners in that he is male, married, and the father of young children. Most of the other emerging Web sites were being set up by young women.

One of the most devoted is Nici Larson, a fifteen-year-old student who lives in Minnesota. She set up her site, geocities.com/nashville/9426/chicks.html, in January 1998, and she quickly became known in Chicks circles as "NicChick."

"I like them because they play their own instruments, and they sound good, too," Larson explains. "I sing and write songs, and I kinda want to do that when I get older, but my mom and dad say I should keep going with the Web sites and keep doing things with computers and I kinda like that, too." Nici says she is self-taught on the computer and learned how to build her Web site by trial and error.

Larson met the Chicks for the first time in mid-1998 when they performed in her hometown of North Mankato, Minnesota. Natalie's husband, Michael, communicated with Nici by e-mail and provided her with e-mail addresses by which she could get in touch with management. To Larson's delight, her e-mail dexterity paid off: She was provided with four tickets and four backstage passes to the concert, which she shared with her mother, Bev, and an Internet friend, Jodie, and her mother.

Unknown to Larson, the band's publicist, Kathy Allmand, contacted Larson's hometown newspaper and convinced them to do a story on the young computer whiz. According to the newspaper, the Chicks decided to check out their Web sites one day while doing a photo shoot for *People* magazine. They discovered Larson's page and, to their delight, found information about their career that was unknown even to them. (The newspaper did not explain what new information they discovered.) Lanie Miller, an executive at the Chicks' record label, told the newspaper that they had been circulating Larson's material around the office and referring people to the Web site.

After the concert, young Larson went backstage to meet the Chicks. It turned into a real ChickFest. As Nici walked in, bearing gifts for her heroines—little boxes filled with Chicklets that had baby chicks on the top—Natalie raised up and shouted, so that everyone in the room could hear, "Hey! It's the Web site girl!" Maines knew what Nici looked like because her photograph had appeared in the local newspaper.

"Emily was pretty shy, but the others talked to me," Larson says of her backstage visit. "They were really nice, and they thanked me a lot for doing my Web site and for helping them out."

In the months that followed, Natalie and Michael stayed in touch with Larson and visited her Internet message board and answered questions posted by fans of the group. Soon everyone associated with the band, including road crew and musicians, were visiting the site and answering questions.

Sixteen-year-old Janelle Hackenbeck, who lives in Red Deer, Alberta,

Canada, explained her devoted interest in the Chicks like this: "They are down-to-earth women and play their own instruments, which is a good thing. They don't let anyone push them down. Some people may see them as blonde women who can't do anything, but they are strong women. They are incredible, and if people would take the time to see them, they would see great people."

Hackenbeck first saw them in person in July 1998, when they performed at the Calgary Stampede in Calgary, Alberta. "I met them after the show," says Janelle. "I had to stand in line for a long time. They were in a bar, and I'm only fifteen and so minors had to leave by three o'clock. But I stayed there without getting caught . . . I was the youngest person there. They did a signing for about one hundred people next to the stage, and that's where I met them and got a T-shirt signed."

The first Chick Janelle spoke to was Natalie. She told the newest Dixie Chick about hiding out in the nightclub and how, because of her age, she feared going to the lady's room, afraid it would give club staff the opportunity to ask her troublesome questions. "She thought that was so funny," says Hackenbeck. "She said, 'You must have had to go to the bathroom so bad.' So then I moved over to Martie and told her, and she thought it was so sweet. I didn't get to talk to Emily."

Several months later, the Chicks returned to Calgary, and Janelle was hopeful of meeting them again. She requested a backstage pass from management, but when she received no response by the day of the concert, she went anyway. With her she carried a picture of Emily she had drawn in her high school art class. When she arrived at the venue, she showed the drawing to a member of the band's entourage, who informed the teenager that she was, indeed, on the list to get in.

"I was so excited and shaky while I stood in line," Janelle remembers. "Everyone was complimenting my picture, and Martie kept smiling at me. I was so shocked at how nice they are. I look up to them so much because I want to be a singer."

When Janelle met Martie, she told her about her career ambitions.

"What kind of singer?" asked Martie.

"Country."

"Right on," said Martie.

Toward the end of the summer, Angie McIsaac, a writer for *Cyber Country*, an Internet music magazine, met the Chicks in Canton, Ohio, when they were making a concert appearance. McIsaac attended the concert not because she was a big fan of the Chicks—she had, in fact, not yet heard any of their four albums—but because it was a family outing with her mother.

"Once I got there and saw the talent, I immediately got interested," she comments. "They are three every talented women. It is amazing to me how well they are doing, with all the problems they've had."

That was all it took for the twenty-five-year-old to become part of the growing Dixie Chicks Internet system. She communicates with other young women by e-mail, and they exchange stories and gossip on the group. They are the foot soldiers of the Dixie Chicks revolution, which, to them, has as much to do with self-discovery (and what it means to be a woman coming of age in the postfeminist era) as it does with country music.

Fourth of July, 1998: The Dixie Chicks were booked at Westfest, an annual country music festival held in Winter Park, Colorado, about a two-hour drive from Denver. Performing with them that day were Jerry Jeff Walker and Junior Brown.

With "Wide Open Spaces" scheduled as the next single to be released, videomaker Thom Oliphant went to Westfest to meet with the Dixie Chicks; he was allocated slightly over three days to capture the essence of the Chicks on the road.

Oliphant traveled with three camera technicians, and he himself operated a fourth camera, which he positioned at the rear of the venue near the sound mixing board. Before leaving Nashville, he sketched out a video that would contain live concert footage and more personal moments on the road.

During the concert, Oliphant was struck with how many different age groups responded to the band. "When you see some shows, you know when some artists walk out on stage, and it all quiets down—and they really had that, but they had it from adults all the way down to nine-year-old little boys and girls who were there with their parents, all going nuts."

Oliphant blended concert footage with scenes photographed on the bus, and punctuated that with an assortment of unpredictable roadside adventures shot in the mountains around Winter Park. "They were so natural," he says. "Anything I would say, they knew what to do by instinct."

When he drove through Denver, he rented a trampoline with the hope that he could find a good use for it as a prop. He had no way of knowing that Martie and Emily had previously relaxed in the recording studio by working out on a trampoline.

"I think the oddest request I had for them was the trampoline," Oliphant observes. "Here's this trampoline sitting in the middle of this dirt road in the middle of nowhere. It was ninety-five degrees outside. They got into it, but leading up to it was funny."

When time came for them to hit the trampoline, Natalie went first, "though that was just because she was ready first." Martie and Emily followed, the childlike excitement showing on their faces despite the heat.

"They are not newcomers [to music]," Oliphant continues. "They've been doing it since they were nine or ten years old. The line that is too far for them is quite a ways out there. They know when to stop, but it takes a while. For a guy who's all about shooting visuals, it is great because you never have to wonder about offending the people you are shooting."

All in all, Oliphant regards working with them on their videos as a great adventure. "Coming from me, saying it is a pleasure to work with somebody is a compliment," he says, laughing, "—and it really was. They are not horrific divas yet, and I hope they never are."

Three months later, the Chicks did a music industry showcase in Los Angeles. "They totally won that room over, too," says Oliphant, who attended the performance. "It was filled with industry people, a tough room, and they totally got them. These were real cynical people, scared to death of losing their jobs [if they made the wrong decisions], and they still loved them."

When *Wide Open Spaces* was first released, Natalie told her bandmates that they needed to do something to celebrate any gold records or Number One hits that came their way. Something symbolic of their success. She suggested they commemorate each gold record and Number One hit with a tiny chicken's foot tattooed on their ankles.

Yeah, fat chance of that, thought Martie and Emily—so they agreed to do it.

By fall 1998, *Wide Open Spaces* had cracked the Top 10 on the album charts, making the Chicks the only new country act that year to do so. They also made the pop album charts, the first country group to do so since 1983, when Alabama placed a Top 10.

For Sony Nashville, it offered an even bigger prize, for it was the first time, ever, that a Nashville-based group had provided the label with a Top 10 pop hit. Album sales quickly reached half a million units, which entitled it to be certified gold. Three months later, sales surpassed the million mark, allowing the album to be certified platinum.

Martie and Emily knew what that meant—tattoos!

Amid much gnashing of teeth—and an occasional groan—the three women went to a Nashville tattoo parlor, where each woman received a tiny chicken-foot tattoo on her ankle. It seemed like a big step, one that carried them light years away from the old retro-cowgirl days when their symbols were Mom, apple pie, and the Star-Spangled Banner.

When the time came for their second round of tattoos, they discovered that the tattoo parlor had gone out of business. After asking around, they learned that one of the tattoo artists, Marty Cade, had moved over to another business named Lone Wolf Tattoos, which was owned by Ben Dixon.

The business is located upstairs over a pizza parlor near Vanderbilt University. The first thing you notice upon entering is a seven-foot mural that is composed of splashy portraits of naked women, fearsome beasts, and metamorphosing human beings. Across from the mural is a fountain with giant goldfish and lush, green foliage. On the walls are dozens of exotic designs for tattoos. Despite the gothic content of some of the wall art, the room has a bright, airy appearance.

One day Martie and her friend, Susan Gibson, who wrote "Wide Open Spaces" for the Chicks, breezed into Lone Wolf without an appointment.

Gibson said that she wanted to get a tattoo on her hand.

"I don't tattoo hands," said Dixon, who didn't recognize Martie. "It would depend on what type of work you are in. It could affect your ability to get a job. What kind do you want?"

Gibson wanted a chicken foot. As if on cue, Martie pulled down her sock and showed Dixon the delicate chicken-foot tattoo on her ankle.

Dixon asked Gibson what she did for a living.

"I'm a songwriter," she said.

"Well, there's lots of songwriters here in Nashville," Dixon said. "You aren't telling me much."

"Really, I've written some good songs," Gibson said. "I don't think I'll have a problem getting one on my hand."

"Well, who have you written songs for? Anyone famous?"
"Yeah, her," she said, pointing to Martie.
"Who are you?" Dixon asked.
"I sing with the Dixie Chicks," Martie said.

Dixon did Gibson's tattoo and touched up Martie's tattoo. If it was a test run, Dixon passed with flying colors. Later, Martie returned with Emily and Natalie. Accompanying them was an entourage made up of Martie's husband, Ted, their producer Paul Worley, and various members of their crew. All wanted chicken-foot tattoos.

"We had a lot of fun," Dixon declares. The only other celebrities he had tattooed were wrestlers from the World Wrestling Federation, and they weren't half as much fun as the Chicks. "After I realized who they were, we closed the shop down, and everybody kicked back and had a good time. Emily seemed more nervous than the others. Martie actually seemed to like it . . . I think she enjoyed the pain a little bit."

Actually, none of the women complained about the pain, says Dixon, although they made "lots of faces" and "little squeaky sounds" during the procedure. Dixon worked on Martie and Emily, and Cade took care of Natalie. They divided up the men, with each tattoo artist taking his share.

Dixon has a beige sofa in his office, and a chair that resembles a barber's chair with an extended leg rest. On the walls are posters of Dracula and various designs for tattoos. Dixon is also a makeup artist and has toy creatures on the wall for inspiration.

Throughout the session with the Chicks, Natalie ran back and forth to Dixon's office, where he was working on Martie and Emily, to make sure that they were all getting identical tattoos. Before doing the tattoos, Dixon drew them on the girls' feet with a pen. If Natalie did not feel it looked right, she would ask him to erase it and try again. "She was like the coordinator," laughs Dixon.

Dixon said the location the Chicks chose is one of the most painful places to apply a tattoo. "Most people get them above the ankle, instead of on the foot," he says. "I told them, the way you're going, you're going to have your whole foot covered. I told them they needed to start thinking about how to do them, maybe coming around their ankles, incorporating them into an anklet. Then we started talking about the future of their careers and how many more tattoos they may end up getting."

The Dixie Chicks had become bona fide "overnight" stars, a fact that was later brought home by awards garnered at the 1998 Country Music Association's annual ceremony held in Nashville each September.

The Chicks took home awards for "Group of the Year" and the Horizon Award, which is given out to the new recording act that has shown the most promise.

As a result of the publicity *Wide Open Spaces* was getting, Natalie was booked on Bill Maher's *Politically Incorrect* late-night television show on ABC. Several days before going on the show, she went to a bingo parlor with Vicki Nash, wife of band guitarist Tommy Nash.

Natalie had cultivated a real passion for bingo. It began only weeks after she joined the Chicks. The band was performing in Shreveport, Louisiana, when Natalie turned twenty-one. That event coincided with Tommy and Vicki Nash's wedding anniversary. Vicki traveled to Shreveport to celebrate with her husband.

As an anniversary gift, the Chicks provided Tommy and Vicki with a complimentary hotel suite. During the visit, Natalie told Vicki that she wanted to learn how to gamble. Vicki took her to one of the local casinos and showed her the ropes.

"I took her to the quarter machines," she confesses. "She was on a machine, and I was on a machine, and I was winning and she was not. She is so competitive. She got so upset with that machine. I said, 'Here take my machine.' She got twenty-five dollars worth of quarters and won maybe seventy-five dollars."

From slot machines, Natalie gravitated to bingo. There was just something about the game that intrigued her. "She's so different playing bingo than she is on stage," says Vicki. "She couldn't even talk, keeping those numbers marked. She couldn't talk. She was sweating. It was just pouring out of her. She was cute."

Of course, by that point Natalie couldn't go into a bingo parlor looking like Natalie. She dressed down big time. "She wore a baseball cap and cut-off jeans and no makeup and looked like a little street girl," says Vicki. "We did that purposely so no one would bug her. I didn't hardly recognize her."

While they were playing bingo, Vicki asked Natalie what she was going to say on *Politically Incorrect*.

"Well," Natalie answered, "they are telling me what to say."

A woman sitting next to Natalie said, "Who's going to be on *Politically Incorrect?*"

"Natalie," said Vicki to the woman.

"No," the woman said.

"Yes, really," Vicki said.

"I don't believe it," said the woman, giving Natalie the once over.

"When we left, I said [to the stranger], 'You watch the show, and you're going to be embarrassed,'" Vicki recounts.

"No, she's not on the show," the woman said, refusing to believe it.

"I kept saying, 'Yes she is,'" says Vicki, "and Natalie looked so embarrassed over the whole thing."

That fall, former Dixie Chicks drummer Tom Van Schaik saw Emily for the first time in a long while, when she attended a concert at which her boyfriend Charlie Robison was opening for Robert Earl Keen (Van Schaik's new employer).

"Emily has this very distinctive laugh—nobody in the world laughs like Emily," says Van Schaik. "I was up on stage finishing up the sound check, and from the back of the stage I heard this laugh. I thought, 'Well, Emily's here.' So we hung out for an hour and a half . . . reminiscing. She said she had only been home four or five days in the past six months. She said they had been so busy, they hadn't had time to relish what they had achieved. I could tell talking to her it was the same ol' Emily. She's just a great girl."

For Van Schaik, the visit brought back old memories of the hard days out on the road with the Dixie Chicks. "The success that they have had so far has surpassed anything I thought they would achieve—it still amazes me," says Van Schaik. "Just a few years ago we were out touring the festival circuit in a RV, and now look at them! I remember the fifteen-hour drives in the back of the van and the air conditioner blowing about ninety degrees. Those were fun times, but they were hard times, too. They put in their time, and they deserve to really do well."

Emily had her own story to tell about her trip to visit Robison. On the flight to Austin, she noticed the in-flight magazine, which was prominently displayed on the back of each seat, had a cover story on the Dixie Chicks.

Every place she looked on the plane, she made eye contact with her own photo. To make matters worse, she felt that the other passengers were looking at the magazine, then looking at her, putting two and two together.

For the "shy" Chick, it was all unnerving. "Let me tell you, I fall asleep on planes with my mouth totally open, and it certainly doesn't look very attractive," Emily told Fred Shuster of the *Los Angeles Daily News*. Now she's got something else to worry about: airplane passengers who recognize her and stalk her, just waiting for her to nod off and provide them with a tabloid photo of the Shy Chick sucking in air like a jet engine.

As the success of the Dixie Chicks increased during 1998, so did the pressures on their management. Robert Brooks, the soft-spoken Dixie Chick fan who set up a Web site to pay tribute to their past, was threatened with legal action by the Dixie Chicks' management if he did not remove thirty-second sound clips from his pages.

Issues of copyright and trademark infringement aside (they are complicated issues and open to various interpretations), attacking a fan whose only goal is to disseminate information about recording artists is most definitely not good public relations, even if the fan is providing the sound clips from the band's archival recordings free of charge.

Because Brooks didn't have money to spend on a lawyer, he removed the sound clips as requested. Picking up on the story was the *Dallas Observer*, which published a feature on December 10, 1998, on the incident under the headline, "Teaching a (history) lesson: Dixie Chicks sic lawyers on a fan's exhaustive web site." Zac Crain wrote: "Brooks didn't mean any harm. He just wanted to let the band's new fans in on what they didn't know they were missing."

A lawyer for the Dixie Chicks told the *Dallas Observer* that the only issue at stake was the ownership of the copyrighted material that was being disseminated over the Internet by Brooks. "It's not fair for him to take their copyright and decide that he's unilaterally going to give it away out on the Internet," the attorney told the newspaper. "It's not fair for him to do that. He may try to cast it as David versus Goliath or Robin Hood or whatever, but it's just not fair for him to do that. He never even asked."

There is merit in that, of course. The Dixie Chicks do own their own recordings, no question about that. The courts have come down squarely on the side of creators of short works such as songs and poems. People can use brief excerpts from books and articles under the "fair use" doctrine without the copyright owner's permission because such usage does not threaten the integrity of the work. By contrast, two lines

All dressed up and everywhere to go.
Courtesy of the author

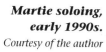

***Martie soloing,
early 1990s.***
Courtesy of the author

Laura plays bass while singing.
Courtesy of the author

Martie, Laura, and Emily with Liza Minnelli.
Courtesy of the author

Laura embraces producer Larry Seyer as Martie and Emily look on and Lloyd Maines plays steel guitar in background.

Courtesy of the author

Dixie Chicks accept the award for best vocal group at the 1998 Country Music Association awards.

Copyright © Alan L. Mayor

Natalie's tattoos.
Copyright © Alan L. Mayor

Emily shows off her tattoos.
Copyright © Alan L. Mayor

***Dixie Chicks hold hands while
getting their tattoos.***
Copyright © Alan L. Mayor

Chicks show off their tattoos.
Copyright © Alan L. Mayor

Internet fan Whitney Israel with Dixie Chicks.
Courtesy of Whitney Israel

Dixie Chicks perform at Country Radio Seminar's
New Faces show.
Copyright © Alan L. Mayor

Emily takes a banjo solo.
Copyright © Alan L. Mayor

As Chicks announce the 1999 Nashville–connected
Grammy nominees, they break out into smiles when they
come upon their own names.

Copyright © Alan L. Mayor

Emily, Martie, and Natalie try on Dallas Cowboys helmets before a Dallas concert. Moments after this photo was taken, there was a commotion when Emily panicked when she got her hair caught in the helmet while removing it.

Courtesy of the author

Emily, Laura, Natalie, and Martie backstage before the concert.

Courtesy of the author

Emily, left, Natalie, and Martie jam on stage in Dallas.
Courtesy of the author

Emily, right, plays dobro, while Lloyd Maines, left, burns up the steel.
Courtesy of the author

Chicks perform "There's Your Trouble" at the Country Music Awards show in 1999.

Copyright © Alan L. Mayor

***Chicks* with Fly producers Blake Chancey
and Paul Worley.**

***Chicks* with Susan Gibson, writer of
"Wide Open Spaces."**

Chicks perform at the Monument Records showcase in Printer's Alley, 1999.

Emily and Martie on stage.
Courtesy of the author

Dixie Chicks accepting the award for best vocal group at the 35th Annual Academy of Country Music Awards, May 3, 2000.
AP/Wide World/Kevork Djansezian

from a poem or song can represent a significant percentage of the work and can represent a threat to the artistic integrity of the song or poem.

Brooks was in error to sample the Chicks music on-line without their permission. However, the band's management did not need to go after the well-meaning Brooks in such a heavy-handed manner. Despite the conflict with management, Robert Brooks has remained a devoted fan of the Dixie Chicks. "I still like them," he says. "They have a sound that is different than anything else coming out of Nashville. That sound has its roots in their long history."

Blake Chancey, the artists and repertoire executive who produced *Wide Open Spaces,* does not think that it is the Dixie Chicks' history that has made them who they are today, but rather their performance style, which blends the acoustic sounds of the banjo and fiddle with a high-energy country format.

"It's their sound, their harmonies, their playing," Chancey told the *Los Angeles Times.* "The sound is more organic—there's less reverb, and the acoustic instruments are more prominent. Nobody else out there sounds like the Dixie Chicks, and that's one of the reasons they're having this success."

By the end of the year, *Wide Open Spaces* had gone triple platinum (three millions units sold). Watching the meteoric rise of the group from the sidelines was Laura Lynch, who ran into Emily toward the end of the year in Dallas.

"I asked Emily what it was like," Laura says, meaning the success. "She said, 'Laura, the grind is the same, the paychecks, the stage, and the audience is way bigger, and the sound system is always good. That's the only difference. The other stuff is all the same."

Laura smiles telling that story. "You know, we used to carry pump bottles of Listerine and spray the microphones to clean them up," she says, her eyes growing bigger. "I swear I got sick off of [dirty] microphones."

10

"I'M IN IT FOR THE MONEY. DIDN'T I TELL Y'ALL THAT?"

1999

Not long after the Dixie Chicks took home their awards from the Academy of Country Music on May 5, 1999, they went to Fort Smith, Arkansas, to perform at the state fair. About three weeks before they arrived, DeAnna Lee, a midday personality on local KTCS radio, began a minute-by-minute countdown to the precise moment the Chicks would arrive in town.

DeAnna Lee falls right in the middle of the demographics that have been key to the band's success. She's female, twenty-six years of age, and she sings, plays guitar, and writes music. In her spare time, she teaches swing dancing at the Grace Dewitt Dance Studio. "I was so excited I could hardly sleep the night before the show," she confesses. "I knew I was going to meet them and could not wait."

On the day of their performance, there was some confusion about her backstage pass, and she was not allowed to enter. Only by being persistent was she able to get past the gatekeepers. Once she did, it was so crowded backstage that she almost did not get in to meet the Chicks. She was told she was too late.

"I almost passed out," she says. "I told the person who I was, and I think he saw the anxiousness in my face. He finally let me go in."

When she came face-to-face with the Dixie Chicks, she was shaking with nervous energy. "I almost cried with joy," she says. "To my surprise, Natalie Maines was my same height. A little squatty body just like me!

"I always tried to pick who I thought was the prettiest in pictures. I would always pick Natalie, Emily, and Martie in that order. It was funny that when I finally saw them face-to-face that order was automatically reversed. Martie has this supermodel glow to her that is so undeniably gorgeous that pictures do not do her enough justice. Natalie is a dork just like me. Silly and full of energy she was."

The Chicks taped a promotional spot for DeAnna Lee's radio station and signed autographs and posed for photographs. "I cried when they started singing because I saw their dream coming true right in front of me. So honest and real . . . I couldn't shut up about it on the radio for weeks after the meeting. I couldn't sleep for two nights after that, thinking, 'Oh, I could have said or done something different.'"

For a different perspective, consider the observations of DeAnna Lee's program director, Ken Michaels. "I think the current Chicks are very intriguing, even though they really don't represent country just like Shania [Twain] doesn't represent country," he believes. "I personally hope that country radio goes back to real country someday."

Michaels first met the Dixie Chicks in the early 1990s while working the afternoon shift at KASE radio in Austin, Texas. "They had a different lead singer at the time," he continued. "They were in town to open for our state at AquaFest. I think the headliner that night was Alan Jackson. Anyway, they were very standoffish and didn't really endear themselves to the people on or off stage that day."

Compared to the ten-year tour of duty Martie and Emily already had put into making the Dixie Chicks a success, Natalie Maines' time investment with the group was minuscule. The differences among the women could not possibly have been greater.

The sisters were tall, glamorous blondes, who endeared themselves to their audiences, while Natalie was diminutive and sometimes displayed a combative personality on stage. The sisters had fallen in love with country music as young children; Natalie was still working at falling in love with it.

The sisters had been raised by teacher-parents and had a healthy respect for social tradition, even if they sometimes strayed in their private lives. Natalie was liable to say anything at anytime, regardless of the consequences, and whenever the Chicks did joint interviews the uncertainty about what Natalie might say was always evident on the sisters' faces. In many ways, Natalie is the archetypal "loose cannon."

Early in 1999, Natalie shocked her friends by filing for divorce from Michael Tarabay, her husband of less than two years. The documents were filed in the Fourth Circuit Court in Nashville and listed the grounds for divorce as irreconcilable differences. Natalie's lawyer, David Garrett, advised the court that both parties expected to enter into a marital dissolution agreement, a prediction that, as it turned out, was overly optimistic.

An attempt to contact Michael through his Nashville-based lawyer, Maclin Davis, revealed that Tarabay had vacated the residence he had shared with Natalie on Warfield Drive in Nashville. No one seemed to know Michael's whereabouts, including his own lawyer. The summons itself was delivered to the office of his lawyer and was signed for by the receptionist. "I have an address where I can write to him," said Davis, "but I can't get in touch with him by telephone."

Natalie remained at the house, a redbrick structure located in an older section of Nashville that is populated with middle-class homes, most of which appear to have been built in the 1950s and 1960s. The house has a double A-frame exterior in the front, with one of the A-frames containing the entrance and the other a bay window. On one end of the house is an open porch, which Natalie has filled with over-stuffed sofas and chairs, giving it a laid-back, retro-hippie ambiance.

There is something about the house, perhaps its use of a double A-frame facade, that resembles the gingerbread houses often described in children's fairy tales. The lawn is neat and tidy, accented with flowering shrubs and well-trimmed trees. The house is not difficult to find if you know the area, but since the street sign that signals the turnoff from the main thoroughfare has mysteriously disappeared, the house is cradled in a protective layer of anonymity.

Rumors about the breakup had been building for months, primarily because of the attention Natalie was receiving from male admirers while on the road. Friends told newspapers that the many love letters she received each day from fans had put unbearable pressures on the marriage. In the beginning, the marriage had been a source of support for her as she entered into uncharted waters; now it seemed like more of a hindrance, something that could only hold her back.

At about this time, the Dixie Chicks introduced a new slogan: "Chicks Rule!" It was a sophomoric attempt to link the Chicks to 1990s-style feminism—and it had a decidedly good ring to it to thirteen- and fourteen-year-olds—but the real genesis of the phrase seemed to be rooted more in Natalie's personality, which seemed to grow more bold and obnoxious with each passing day.

In an interview with Laura Jamison for *Seventeen* magazine, Natalie said she had jumped at the chance to join the band, but told the sisters she would not wear the retro-cowgirl clothes they had used for years. Natalie laughed retelling the story to the reporter. "But they were ready for a change anyway."

"We were really looking for a soul sister," said Emily. "Someone who was in it for the music."

"I'm in it for the money," cracked Natalie. "Didn't I tell y'all that?"

The sisters laughed at Natalie's wisecrack, but it was probably nervous laughter, for, to them, their music was their first priority in life. Interestingly, in the same issue of *Seventeen* that carried the interview was a double-page advertisement for Candie's athletic shoes that featured the Dixie Chicks. It was their first major endorsement since Natalie joined the group.

In the photo, Natalie bends over, bracing herself with her outstretched arms, as Martie reaches down and appears to give her a wedgie by yanking up her underwear. Seated in a nearby chair, Emily tilts her head back, laughing as she holds what could pass for a retro-cowgirl hat in place.

Natalie, Martie, and Emily showed up at the forty-first annual Grammy Awards ceremony on February 24, 1999, at Shrine Auditorium in Los Angeles, looking like anything but retro-cowgirls.

They each wore black outfits, studded with dozens of safety pins. Natalie wore a miniskirt and a jacket, Martie wore a skirt slit all the way up to her hips, and Emily wore a black vest with an upturned collar. Both sisters sported bare midriffs.

Commenting on the outfits in *US* magazine, Joe Bob Briggs, of TNT's *MonsterVision,* said, "We don't have to guess which Chick has midriffphobia, do we?" Comedian Cathy Ladman made the observation that the women's outfits were "the result when Satan markets a line of clothing for Kmart."

Nominated for Grammys in the categories of Best New Artist, Best Country Performance by a Duo or Group with Vocal, and Best Country Album, the Dixie Chicks took home awards for Best Country Performance by a Duo or Group with Vocal, beating out Alabama, BR5-49, the Mavericks, and the Wilkinsons, and for Best Country Album, winning against Garth Brooks, Faith Hill, Shania Twain, and Trisha Yearwood.

The Chicks did not win the Best New Artist award, but they were honored to be the only country artists included in the same category with pop sensations Backstreet Boys, Andrea Bocelli, Lauryn Hill, and Natalie Imbruglia. It was the Best Country Album award that came as a complete shock to everyone, including the Chicks, for it had been assumed by most critics that Shania Twain would win.

While on stage to accept the award in the album category, Martie said, "We thought for sure that Shania got it. She just performed, and we thought that was the way you win." Said Natalie: "We got to break Nashville's rules and do what we wanted to do—they let us play our instruments." So, who says Chicks don't wear spurs?

The Dixie Chicks were enjoying an unprecedented run of good luck. Within the space of several months they had won two Grammys, two Country Music Association Awards, and an American Music Award for Favorite New Artist (Country).

For months, *Wide Open Spaces* had held first or second place on the country album charts and had cracked the Top 10 on the pop charts. By early summer 1999, the album had sold more than five million units and established the Dixie Chicks as the best selling country group of 1998. Incredibly, the album sold more units than all other country groups combined in 1998.

In its December 24, 1998, double issue, *Rolling Stone* magazine raved about the band: "The Dixie Chicks were the badass queenpins of country this year, ruling the radio with their crazy sexy cool . . . they were country's finest proponents of high-spirited thrills."

Outside of performances on industry award shows, the Dixie Chicks were still largely unknown to most television viewers. Before performing on the American Music Awards in Los Angeles on January 10, 1999, the Chicks were admittedly nervous.

"We've performed for a TV audience before," Natalie told *TV Guide*, "but we've always had the safety net of country music. Now we'll have to prove ourselves to our peers in other genres of music."

At the award ceremony, where they were nominated for Favorite New Artist (Country), the Dixie Chicks performed their hit, "Wide

Open Spaces," backed by their touring band and Papa Maines playing steel guitar in the background. Nominated in the same category with the Dixie Chicks were the Kinleys and the Wilkinsons, but when the winner was announced by Toby Keith and Randy Travis, it was the Dixie Chicks who took the stage.

"Just like they say in country music—Yee-Haw!" said Natalie. "We want to thank Monument Records and country radio, and all our fans especially for buying our records. And our dogs and our cats, and who else?"

"Our husbands," said Martie.

"And our management," said Emily.

"Our makeup artists and our hair stylists," said Natalie, "because that's what it's all about."

The first long-form television introduction to the Dixie Chicks was on *Austin City Limits* on February 13, 1999, which allowed the women to split the sixty-minute show with Emily's fiancé, Charlie Robison. Of course, there was more to the booking than met the eye. Sony Nashville had made a side deal with Papa Maines to produce an album on Charlie Robison. Not surprisingly, Maines performed with both acts that night.

"Well, how many chicks do we have out there tonight?" Natalie shouted to the audience when she took the stage. "Well, this song goes out to all the chicks out there 'cause we're the only ones who know how hard it is to find that man . . . so fellows I'm gonna take it upon myself to speak on behalf of all chicks, and it would be right good for you to play close attention."

With that, Maines launched into a blues song that allowed her to dip into the guttural vocals that other country artists—such as Wynonna—have tried and failed to deliver for years. Natalie handled it just fine.

"That's my sister getting on the banjo—that's Emily ya'll," says Martie. "When you're growing up in Texas and you're a banjo picker, you're not always the most popular girl in school . . . Anyway, I love to feature her . . . she's such an awesome banjo picker."

Martie and Emily launched into "Little Roanoke," an up-tempo instrumental that features battling banjo and fiddle. Watching them perform together on an instrumental in which each player takes a turn and then joins in to play together is as much visual entertainment as it is auditory. They have a way of dragging the listener into their special world, which, when you get right down to it, is what the best music is all about.

On May 5, 1999, the Dixie Chicks dominated the thirty-fourth annual Academy of Country Music Awards at the Universal Amphitheatre in Los Angeles by winning awards as the top new vocal duet or group, top duet or group, and the coveted album of the year.

They were expected to take home the award for top new duet or group, but winning an award for top duet or group, which had been dominated by Brooks and Dunn in recent years, and, more important, album of the year, was a total surprise.

"It's great to win the Brooks and Dunn," joked Natalie from the stage. "It's beautiful!"

Earlier, when they won the top duet or group award, edging out Sawyer Brown, Brooks and Dunn, and the Wilkinsons, the women, who were dressed as orange, pink, and green flamingos, took turns thanking everyone from radio to their record label.

Emily thanked ACM leader Dick Clark and his top production executive, Gene Weed. Before they left the stage, Maines tossed a thank you of her own: "We want to thank Charlie Robison because we never thought anyone would marry Emily."

Backstage, Dick Clark interviewed the women and explained to the television audience that Emily had been married to Robison only a few days earlier. Emily said that Martie and Natalie had come into the bedroom the night after they got married and crashed the honeymoon. It was no joke.

When it was announced that the Dixie Chicks had won the award for album of the year, winning over Shania Twain, Faith Hill, and others, the women seemed totally shocked. Martie had tears in her eyes as she took the stage. Natalie cried out, "Oh, my god!" And Emily said, "We'd be lying if we said we didn't want this one."

Of the three Chicks, it was obviously Emily who had fallen in over her head in a dream world. On May 1, only days before the Academy of Country Music event, she and Charlie Robison had exchanged marriage vows at a 25,000-acre ranch near Dallas.

There were no airports nearby, so many of the two hundred guests had to be flown in on private airplanes. Once the guests arrived, they were checked out by Texas state troopers who matched their invitations with their driver's licenses. All the hotel rooms for miles around were booked for the guests, many of whom were Sony executives.

With Martie and Natalie as her bridesmaids—and Charlie's brother Bruce as best man—Emily became the last of the Chicks to relinquish her never-married status. Afterward the women sang "Cowboy, Take Me Away," and later Natalie and Martie, still dressed in their bridesmaids' dresses, were unceremoniously tossed into the swimming pool by the guests.

The night following the Academy of Country Music awards, the Dixie Chicks made an appearance on CBS television's *Late, Late Show* with Craig Kilborn. Sitting in the chair closest to Kilborn's desk, Natalie chastised the host for confusing the Academy of Country Music awards with the Country Music Association awards (one is based in Nashville, and the other is in Los Angeles).

Fans of the group must have been shocked by Natalie's appearance. Whether she had gorged herself on food following the ACM awards or had simply pulled an unfortunate choice in dresses from her closet, she seemed swollen at her midsection and for most of the show sat with her arms folded over her puffy stomach. Sudden weight gains had plagued her from an early age, contributing to the natural pain of adolescence; how painful those old memories must have been to her that night, now that she had become a star, for she clutched her midsection as if she were protecting a secret.

As Natalie continued to toss off smart-aleck comments, it was Martie who seemingly struggled to keep the interview on an even keel. Kilborn seemed confused about what it meant to "cross over" in country music, and Martie used his question to explain why the band was not featured on VH-1. She said they were told their videos would be aired if they took her fiddle out of the pictures—"and we didn't want to do it." Craig good-naturedly asked them if the ultimate goal of country music artists was to get booked on *Hee Haw*.

It was not the Chicks' finest hour.

Danielle Syx is a twenty-six-year-old Birmingham, Alabama, woman who owns her own silk screening and embroidery business. She has been a fan of the Dixie Chicks since meeting them as a teenager. Soft-spoken and reserved, she seems somewhat embarrassed by her devotion to the band, but not so embarrassed that she would not drive to the ends of the earth to attend one of their concerts.

On this day, she has driven to Nashville from Birmingham to link up with "CC," a much younger Chicks fan she met on the Dixie Chicks e-mail group. Together they will drive to Columbus, Ohio, with other fans to attend a Chicks concert.

For Syx, the Internet has become a vehicle for making new friends and for communicating with individuals who have the same interests. "You meet a lot of nice people that way," she affirms. "They are interested in the same thing you are. You can find out about their experiences, who is going to be at the shows, things you wouldn't normally find out."

Syx says it annoys her that some people insist the Dixie Chicks are successful because of their looks. "I beg their pardon because I have witnessed two of them working their tails off to get where they are today—and I have heard Natalie sing," says Danielle. "Natalie has to be one of the best singers in country music. If someone says that these girls are where they are today for the reasons I stated, then apparently someone is lacking the ability to hear the musical and vocal talent that the three ladies have. . . . I am very proud of them, and I think my admiration and love for their music is a lot stronger than it would be for any other musicians because I have witnessed how these girls [Martie and Emily] pushed and pushed and bust their bottoms to accomplish what they have today."

Cynthia Wagner, who likes to be called "CC" or the Texas Spaz, the friend with whom Danielle is traveling to Ohio, seems to have patterned her life after "Wide Open Spaces." At the start of 1999, she dropped out of college in Texas, loaded up her car and drove to Nashville, where she landed a job as a waitress in a mid-town restaurant. In her spare time, the blonde humanitarian works on a Habitat for Humanity project.

Wagner first saw the Chicks on *Prime Time Country,* a program that once aired nightly on TNN. Later, she attended one of the group's Texas concerts and heard them perform live. Before the concert began, she sent a note backstage to the Chicks and signed it the "Texas Spaz."

"I waited for about twenty minutes," she recalls. "I thought, 'Oh, please' . . . five minutes later this guy comes up and he says, 'Are you Cynthia?' and I grabbed my roommate and ran downstairs, and we were waiting in line and I was freakin' out. Finally, it was just the Chicks looking at me and my roommate and I hear 'Who's the Spaz?' and I said, 'Oh, that one, the quiet one, acting real dorky . . . and they said, 'Oh, it's you.'

"I asked Natalie if she took Dramamine and she said, 'No, why?'" continues Wagner. "On my note to the Chicks I put this drawing of my tattoo, a butterfly . . . while I was there they signed the lyrics of 'Wide Open Spaces.' I said, 'I cut my hair and I'm going to drop out of school and I got a tattoo . . . I showed it to them and Emily said, 'That's the tattoo on the note,' and I said, 'Yeah, you're very observant.'"

Wagner showed the author her fan book. It contains all the covers of the previous CDs, various photographs, and concert artifacts such as ticket stubs. She clearly put a lot of work into it. To her, the Dixie Chicks are not so much a musical group as they are a beacon to an alternative way of life.

When I (the author) first met Wagner, it was in the Nashville restaurant where she works. As it happened, it was she who showed me to my table. Not knowing the identity of the hostess, I asked if there was anyone working there named Cynthia Wagner.

"Why, what's she done?" she answered.

I explained that I was not serving a warrant.

"Oh, in that case, it's me," she said.

When the waiter came over to take my order, Wagner introduced me by saying, "This is my father."

"No you're not," the waiter said.

I nodded, but before I could reply, Wagner offered another explanation: "He's not really my father. He owns a strip club and wants me to work for him."

The waiter's eyes widened. At last, here was a story he could believe. Although the restaurant was crowded, he sat down at the table. Wagner sat down as well.

"So," the waiter said, nodding his head in anticipation of an explanation.

"I don't really own a strip club," I said. "I'm writing a book."

"I should write a book myself," said the waiter. "I once went into this strip club in San Francisco . . ."

Before leaving for Ohio with Syx for the Dixie Chicks concert, Wagner gave a tour of the apartment that she and her female roommate share with another woman. She sleeps in a bedroll on the floor of a second story walk-up apartment located within sight of the interstate. She has a computer in her room, but little else. In another era, she could have passed for a cowgirl living out on the range.

Across the country, in Greensboro, North Carolina, twenty-year-old Whitney Israel is on the move in search of the Chicks. The part-time student, who has a Web page dedicated to the band (www.geocities. com/nashville/opry/5727), first saw the Dixie Chicks in concert in September 1998 in Columbia, South Carolina.

When she learned they were performing at Greensboro later that month, she bought tickets to that concert as well. Says Israel: "I became a fan of the Dixie Chicks the first time I heard their first song, 'I Can Love You Better.' I became an avid fan, recording every television appearance, collecting anything that even mentioned the Chicks, and eventually creating a Web page dedicated to the girls." By June 1999, Israel's Web site had received almost 90,000 hits.

When she arrived in Greensboro—her home is in Greenville, South Carolina—she met a group of friends at a local hotel. They planned to hang out in the lobby until time to go to the concert. While they were talking, something happened that sent their blood racing.

"While we were sitting in the lobby, Martie walked in," Israel recalls. "She had been working out, and she had on a baseball hat. I didn't recognize her at first, but one of my friends did. At about that time, Martie recognized that we recognized her, so she just ran out of the lobby, and we went chasing after her calling out her name, but she never turned around. After that, we went walking around looking for more Chicks. We saw Emily in the weight room, but we didn't get to talk to her."

At the concert later that evening, Israel and her friends attended a meet-and-greet for the band. Says Israel: "We gave Martie a cup from the hotel to sign. When we gave it to her, she burst out laughing, and said, 'Oh, you're the girls from the hotel!'

"Though they were obviously tired, they were incredibly nice and sweet to me and my friends," she says. "Natalie said she actually remembered me from the first time we met. (I don't know if she really did, but hey! I was talking to a Dixie Chick so I really didn't care.) They were down-to-earth people, and we ended up chatting for about ten minutes.

"For a moment I forgot that we were talking to the Dixie Chicks," Israel continues. "We just talked about 'stuff,' and they seemed like life-long friends. Not only are they extremely talented musically, but they are just great individuals who really care about their fans. And that's really important. Meeting and actually having a conversation with them ranks up there on my 'Greatest Experiences List.' They are honestly dedicated to their music and fans, which shows. I think that's what makes people like them the way they do. They rock!"

A young girl, who identifies herself only as Lacy from Georgia, claims she is among the biggest Dixie Chicks fans of them all. Not only has she seen them in concert, she has "their tape, their poster, an iron-on, mousepad, T-shirt, 8 x 10 picture, and guitar pick." At a concert at Six Flags in Georgia she saw them perform on the bill with Lee Ann Womack, the Kinleys, and Kevin Sharp.

"I went with a friend and we made a sign, 'Let 'er Rip, Chicks . . . P.S. Natalie–John Travolta!'" Lacy reports. "She likes John and so do I. Well, we moved up closer to the sixth row because we were way in the back. My friend and I took out the poster, and Emily noticed it first and smiled, then Martie smiled, too, and Natalie tried to figure out what it said because of the lights.

"I remember that concert so well. I remember the jokes and everything. We stayed after and tried to meet them, but could not. We did, however, get picks that were Natalie's. The cleanup crew gave them to us—yep, we stayed late."

11

DIXIE CHICKS FLY INTO NEW MILLENNIUM

Amid all the hurly-burly of the 1999 music award shows, the Dixie Chicks maintained a busy concert schedule by touring with veteran country star George Strait and by working on a new album, one that would determine whether the women are one-hit wonders or recording artists with staying power.

"So far we've recorded three originals," Natalie told *Country Weekly* early in 1999. "It's a creative process, and we hope everyone likes it. But we'll definitely be proud of whatever we put out."

Wide Open Spaces had only one song composed by the Chicks—Martie and Emily's "You Were Mine"—but Natalie said the new album, entitled *Fly,* would feature more of their own compositions. "We're new writers and writing our own songs is something we want to do more of."

Martie told *US* magazine that they went on weeklong retreats, during which they directed all their efforts toward writing songs. "We got away and really focused. I think that really helped." Natalie said they wanted to put out a "killer second album." The only thing they hoped to do differently in the year 2000, says Martie, is add a bit of luxury for themselves to their tour and to headline their own concerts instead of opening for other people.

Drummer Greg Morrow, one of the session players who worked on *Wide Open Spaces,* was called back to help put down tracks for *Fly.* Interviewed prior to the release of *Fly,* Morrow would not comment on the album's content other than to hint that the women had kept up the good work.

"A lot of times vocalists come into the studio and they, maybe, only heard the song the day before," he says. "The Dixie Chicks knew their material when they walked in the door. They are confident in what they are doing. That experience really comes out in the studio. They're very professional. They're still eager and hungry. They just love to play. Natalie sings every take like it's her take. Martie and Emily do the same thing. It's not a matter of, 'We did our stuff, and then they [the sessions players] take their turn.'"

As they were working on *Fly*, producer Larry Seyer approached the girls about recording a song for an album he was doing with Asleep at the Wheel. The album, entitled *Drive with Bob* was released in July 1999 and featured guest artists such as Clint Black, Reba McEntire, Vince Gill, and Merle Haggard.

Seyer thought it would be a nice touch for the Dixie Chicks to record a song, "Roly Poly," that was a concert favorite of the Chicks back in the early 1990s.

"Their playing was incredible," he says. "The girls are just great."

Lilith Fair was the brainchild of Canadian recording artist Sarah McLachlan, who established the all-female concert tour as a tribute to the contributions of women in music. The first tour kicked off the day after Independence Day, July 5, 1997, and was repeated again in 1998, offering nearly forty coast-to-coast performances and showcasing more than sixty female artists.

Lilith Fair featured different recording artists in each city and proved to be an enormous creative and financial success. More than 800,000 people attended the 1998 concert series. Most of the audience members were female, and each estrogen-fest seemed to offer proof that America had, indeed, undergone a quiet revolution in popular music, one that began with rocker Melissa Etheridge in the late 1980s.

"You know what the bottom line was?" McLachlan asked Roger Catlin of the *Hartford Courant*. "I just thought it would be really fun to put a whole bunch of women on stage—all the women I loved [to listen to]. To be able to play with them on the same stage and be able to put on a show like that—for us and the audience."

Pat Benatar, who played two dates with the 1997 tour, says the differences among the women of the 1990s and the women of the 1980s (her generation) are nothing short of remarkable. "There is a total difference between their generation and our generation," she explains. "We didn't have that feeling of friendship. We felt like we were competing against each other. We were terrified to let our guard down, of being gentle, kind, any of those things—because it wasn't about that. It was about being as strong as you could to get through it. These women are the product of what we did to get through it."

Donna Westmoreland, concourse manager for Lilith Fair, told *Pulse* magazine that Lilith was a kinder, gentler rock festival than America was used to seeing: "We're trying to make it a little less about debauchery and more about community." Picking up on that was the *New York Times*, whose headline for a feature on the festival read: "Forget the Hard Rock: It's Support for Sisterhood."

"Like a lot of good ideas, the Lilith Fair already seems inevitable," wrote Jon Pareles for the *New York Times*. "Sooner or later, someone was bound to put together two 1990s phenomena: The surging commercial fortunes of female songwriters and the summer package tour as reinvented by the Lollapalooza Festival."

Sarah McLachlan told Pareles she was more than happy to oblige: "If I hadn't done it, somebody else would have. But it was a selfish thing. I never got to see the people I love playing live."

Texas pop singer Abra Moore, who played five dates with the 1997 tour, said then that although Lilith's success was part of the "balancing out" of American music, it was going to require more from female artists than simply showing up.

"It's all been said, you know what I mean? Everyone is out there interpreting their own creative vision. As far as being a female artist, what is it that I have to say that is new? I don't know how to answer that." Moore broke into laughter. "Maybe that gives you some insight into my world."

When the time came to release the schedule for the 1999 tour, McLachlan had two surprises: first, that it would be the last Lilith Fair tour, and, second, that coheadliners would be the Dixie Chicks, the Pretenders, and Monica.

"We want to end the tour on a high note," says McLachlan in a press release issued by the Dixie Chicks' record label. "From the beginning, we had a three-year plan. It's a lot of fun, but it is also a lot of work."

Asked by *Elle* magazine if there were no women she would trust to take over Lilith Fair, McLachlan said, "It's not just the woman, it's the organization behind the woman—the management and record company. If I didn't have control, I'd lose my mind, because I have a very particular vision, and my name is associated so strongly with Lilith. Someone should start something new."

Seemingly delighted that there would be no additional Lilith Fair concerts after 1999 was the Reverend Jerry Falwell's newspaper, the *National Liberty Journal*. Two weeks before the 1999 tour kicked off, senior editor J. M. Smith wrote a blistering attack on the tour in its "Parent Alert" column. Smith said in the article: "Many young people no doubt attend the Lilith Fair concerts not knowing the demonic legend of the mystical woman whose name the series manifests."

The *National Liberty Journal* was not the only publication to criticize the festival. So did *Entertainment Weekly,* which offered a tour guide to its readers in its July 16 issue which suggested that concertgoers wear "hairy pits" and a "henna tattoo" to the festival.

The entertainment magazine's jab, written by Rob Brunner and Laura Morgan, was good-natured and, no doubt, meant in a humorous way, but it probably annoyed festival organizers who battled charges for two years that the concerts were being attended mainly by lesbians (as if lesbians didn't have the same right to party and dance as everyone else).

Three weeks earlier, the same magazine did a feature that focused on the fashion, hair, and makeup stylists who attended to the Chicks' growing image as glamorous country divas. Martie described the stylists as the "Glam Squad."

When the magazine questioned the stylists about what the Chicks would be wearing over the summer months, they responded: "Hard Candy lipstick (Tramp), capris, and anything hot pink or army green." Interestingly, the feature article also included a photograph of Laura Lynch performing with Martie and Emily as part of the magazine's "before and after" comparison.

For their part, the Dixie Chicks were delighted to help deliver the tour's swan song and ignored the attacks against them by the Religious Right. Besides, they already had the tattoos and did not mind if the public speculated about the condition of their arm pits. For the Chicks, headlining the festival was an honor. A handful of country artists had appeared on stage from time to time during its previous two runs, but never had a country act headlined the tour.

"Lilith Fair was created to be a celebration of women in music, and no women have been more celebrated in the past year than the Dixie Chicks," said tour organizer Marty Diamond in a press release. "We've enjoyed great performances on the Fair in previous years by artists like Martina McBride, Emmylou Harris, and Mary Chapin Carpenter. Having the Chicks as a principle act, however, gives the tour a little bit different and exciting principal slant. When we approached them, they accepted a headline slot with the stipulation that we offer country radio active participation in the shows, and we look forward to that."

"Some people in the music industry and in the press are asking us if we're trying to 'cross over,' like it's now expected if you reach a certain level of success, which is crazy to me," said Natalie in a press release. "The answer is quite simply, 'No.' We have no plans to ask any other radio format to play our records. Country music is our heritage, it's what we are, and what we will continue to be."

"Music fans and the country music industry are being so supportive of us, that we not only are feeling responsible for growing our particular fan base but also to help keep country music growing as a whole," says Emily in a press release. "Hopefully, us being on the Lilith Fair is one good way to achieve both."

The Dixie Chicks joined the tour on July 15, 1999, in San Diego and stuck with it through the end of August, after which they began promoting their new album, *Fly*. The first single from it, "Ready to Run," was released in July and featured in the Julia Roberts–Richard Gere movie, *Runaway Bride*.

Early in 1999, former Chicks drummer Tom Van Schaik was on a tour bus when someone entered, saying, "Hey, you heard the Chicks are breaking up?" The man went on to say that Natalie was rumored to be unhappy working as part of a trio.

"I hope she doesn't leave, because they've got a chemistry here," says Van Schaik. "Every lead singer in any band, from Restless Heart to Highway 101, who goes out on their own runs into trouble. I hope the rumors are not true. They have so much more they can do as a band. It would be a travesty."

Vicki Nash agrees. "I think it would be the end of the Dixie Chicks," she believes. "What they have is a special thing. A lot of people come to [Natalie], I am sure, and say, 'You can do it yourself.' I don't think [leaving] would be a wise move. If it's not broke, don't fix it. She seems to be happy." Her husband Tommy comes in off the road, she says, with descriptions of the women "just walking on clouds."

Van Schaik pauses, thinking about the possibilities. "Natalie's what? Twenty-two," he laughs. "At twenty-two you're still invincible. I don't know what's going on in her head. They are like the freshest thing out of Nashville, just the sound and the personalities. It'd be a shame to just have this success. I'm looking forward to their follow-up albums, to see where they are going with it. Till the day I die, I will always follow them. They are family at this point."

Angie McIsaac, the Internet music writer who went from "Chicks Who?" to one of the legions of on-line admirers, said she, too, had heard rumors that Natalie might leave the group. "I wouldn't be all that surprised," she stated in a 1999 interview. "Egos start getting in the way . . . I would say that Martie is the most talented. As long as she didn't leave, they would be OK. There's all kinds of women singers who could take [Natalie's] place. There's talent everywhere."

The biggest problem the Dixie Chicks have had to overcome to date has been their name, along with the sexual stereotypical imagery it conjures, and their "blondes have more fun" stage persona. "When you're three blonde women in this industry, you're at a disadvantage as far as perceptions go," Martie told *Seventeen* magazine.

Emily agrees. "It's like, 'Oh, here's another girl group somebody put together,'" she says. "But that's us playing on the CD. A lot of people in Nashville sing over tracks laid down by studio musicians. I may not be the best banjo player in Nashville, but I can re-create our sound in a live show."

"Someone wrote us a letter saying we've put women back generations by calling ourselves chicks," Martie told *Seventeen*. "Women don't have to be so defensive anymore. Just work hard, do what you do best, and reap the rewards."

"Call me a blonde, but I never even thought about the name being sexist," says Natalie to the *Los Angeles Daily News*. "I was thinking about little baby chicks—and that Little Feat song 'Dixie Chicken.' It was totally tongue in cheek. One thing's for sure, it sticks in people's minds. And that was the goal—to be remembered."

"We got a lot of critical acclaim in the beginning, and people saw that the music was good and not just three blondes who were put together like the Monkees or something," says Emily. "There were people who bought the album because they were curious—and that word of mouth really helped, especially among the younger fans."

Natalie likes to point out that lots of bands put out records and are then never heard from again, something she says won't happen with the Dixie Chicks. Martie is more cautious. "There's no guarantee that won't happen to us," Martie told *People* magazine. "I feel like right now is the good old days. I think right now is the proving stage, to prove that we're for real."

One of the things they have picked up from their youngest fans is the perception that the band, especially Natalie, is a little on the wild and crazy side. One reason for that are the road stories about the group that filter back to the fans. Stories about wild food fights. Stories about pajama parties at which the women really let down their hair. Then there is the story about the time the women ganged up on a crew member and held him down on the floor to smear his face with lipstick.

Martie laughs when she talks about Natalie, who she admits is a little "wild and crazy." What the band tries not to do, she says, is take themselves too seriously.

Cary Banks, the instructor at South Plains College in Levelland, Texas, who once played in the Maines Brothers Band, says the success of the Dixie Chicks has had a phenomenal effect on the school's enrollment. Now students want to attend the same school that Natalie attended. That's fine with him. He thinks their music program compares to those offered anywhere.

Even Banks, the seasoned old pro, is proud of his relationship with Papa Maines and Natalie. "She's one in a million," he beams. "In Natalie, more than anyone I've ever seen, all the elements came together. Her genetics, her environment. Plus, she was in the right place at the right time. It was like it was destined to happen."

Cary Banks also gives credit to the record company that released *Wide Open Spaces.* "I was impressed that [the Chicks] were given the artistic freedom they had on the first album. I understand the girls went in and said, 'This is what we want to do. If you guys want to do it fine, if you don't, we'll go down the street.'

"These girls are extremely talented, business oriented, everything it takes to stay on top, but the business is so unpredictable. As long as the Chicks are cool, they'll sell records. If they are hanging all their hopes on the first album, I sure hope they're not disappointed. If their next album only goes platinum, they're going to feel a let down. Critics will say, 'What happened to the Chicks?'"

As 1999 progressed, the Chicks had reason to think their professional prospects would only grow brighter. In mid-June, during a live telecast from the Nashville Arena, the band received even more honors, this time from the TNN Music City News Awards. The Dixie Chicks won in two categories: Female Star of Tomorrow and Vocal Band of the Year.

With record sales at six million and still rising (industry insiders have told the author that no one would be surprised if *Wide Open Spaces* eventually hit the ten million mark), the Dixie Chicks have every reason to be optimistic.

On the occasion of the album hitting the six million sales mark, Sony executive Mike Kraski said: "The Dixie Chicks have a musical appeal that cuts across all musical boundaries and age divisions. Their music is firmly rooted in country and yet what they do is so contemporary and unique, that it is not limited to any one genre."

As if to punctuate that, the Dixie Chicks participated in a fashion spread, along with several other country and pop artists, in the July 1999 issue of the trendy *In Style* magazine. "The trio's flirtatious appearance flies in the face of old-time country's froufrou costumes," noted the magazine. "Self-proclaimed 'girlie' girls, they love experimenting with makeup."

In the accompanying photos, Natalie showed off a firmer midriff, though she did seem to be gritting her teeth somewhat, as if she was holding her breath. Martie told the magazine that they deliberately use "a lot of glitter around the eyes, and extreme hair," so that they will show up from the stage.

Aside from staying together as a band, the biggest challenge facing the Chicks will be their ability to maintain personal relationships outside the band. Martie's husband, Ted Seidel, quit his job with the pharmaceutical company to go on the road with his wife and to be a househusband for his son, Carter. Industry insiders marveled at his dedication: Not many show business marriages survive the schizophrenic mixture of intense closeness and intense distance that comes with stardom.

Emily's union with Charlie Robison offers dynamics of a different sort. Couples who marry within the business and maintain busy touring schedules rarely have time to devote to each other. Emily and Charlie purchased a house in Bandera, Texas, near the home of Robison's parents, but whether they will ever spend much time there together remains to be seen. By July 1999, Emily had sold her house on Van Ness Street in Dallas, severing that part of her life.

From all appearances, Emily and Charlie were a perfect match. But there were danger signs before the year had even ended. Charlie's career didn't take off as quickly as expected, one reason being his reluctance to do interviews with reporters not approved by the Chicks organization. In effect, he put his own career on the back burner so that he could be supportive of Emily's career. A little bit of sacrifice goes a long way in the music business, especially when one partner is more successful than the other.

Natalie made a preemptive strike against marital unhappiness by filing for divorce from Michael Tarabay, but whether that means she has shown foresight in ending a relationship before it became entirely unpleasant or is reacting to the stress of stardom is unknown. The stress generated by the divorce proceedings was evident throughout the year, particularly during the band's performances.

At one of the Lilith Fair tour dates at the Pasadena Rose Bowl, Natalie lost her cool and ranted about her ex from the stage. "The last thing he [Michael] said was, 'It's not about the money,'" she said, according to reporters who seemed stunned to see her air dirty laundry in public. "Seven months later, we're still not divorced, and it's still not about the money . . . I haven't quite figured out what it is about. But what I do know is that with all the money he's gonna take, I'm gonna try and make some more."

July 4, 1999, should have been a time of celebration for the Dixie Chicks. Instead, it was a weekend of betrayal, heartbreak, and dashed dreams.

Without warning, the Chicks fired longtime guitarist Tommy Nash and bassist Bobby Charles Jr. For Nash, who had been with the band since 1995, it came as a total shock. They had just returned from a brief concert engagement in Europe and were preparing for the Lilith Fair summer tour.

From his home just two days after his firing, Nash said he did not want to discuss his status with the band. He was polite but low-keyed, and there was a sadness in his voice that was completely understandable. Nash is an extraordinarily talented guitarist, but job hunting for a man in his fifties is never easy, even among top musicians. Nash and Charles may have been the first casualties of the European tour, but they certainly would not be the last.

The European tour had been stressful and fractious, especially for Martie and Ted, who had engaged in heated arguments within earshot of band members. Perhaps it was only petty bickering, the sort of thing that happens from time to time in all marriages, but if it was serious, then it could have a devastating effect on the group. Martie's friends crossed their fingers and hoped for the best.

The Dixie Chicks' trail is littered with discarded musicians, associates, and partners. Most, like Laura Lynch, David Skepner, and Tom Van Schaik, continue to support the band. Some, like Robin Macy, who today lives in Kansas, where she spends much of her time tending a garden, refuse to discuss the Chicks or their experiences with the band. Old dreams sometimes die hard.

By the time *Fly* was released in September 1999, record company executives were on edge. The album was markedly different from the wildly successful *Wide Open Spaces*. Musically, it was skewed more toward old-time country music than the previous album. Lyrically, it reflected the polar opposite emotions being experienced by Emily, who found love, and Natalie, who descended into the hellfire of divorce.

"Emily's wedding and Natalie's divorce set the whole tone," Martie told Tom Roland of the Nashville *Tennessean*. "My head was spinning. I didn't know what to think, whether to be happy for Emily or crying with Natalie."

In the weeks before the official release of the album, record executives, producers, and management tried to cover their bets by throwing themselves at the media in an effort to "explain" the content of the new album.

In retrospect, it is easy to see why they were concerned.

In addition to the song content, the artwork seemed destined to raise eyebrows. One photo shows the Chicks, with eyes crossed, peering at plastic flies perched on their noses. Another shows them in black leather (or vinyl) stuck to a cylinder of flypaper. Yet another depicts them emerging from a vaginalike slit in a pair of blue jeans.

"Obviously, I'm biased, but I was absolutely blown away," manager Simon Renshaw told *Billboard.* "From an artistic point of view, it shows enormous growth. They're writing more, and I think we're just seeing the tip of the iceberg there."

Sony Nashville president Allen Butler told interviewers that *Fly* had received a boost by being on the soundtrack of the Julia Roberts movie, *Runaway Bride.* Coproducer Chancey said that, going into the studio, they knew the success of the previous album had "set the bar high" for them, but he was happy with the result.

Two songs in particular seemed to concern everyone: "Goodbye Earl," which is about a woman who murders her lover with the help of her girlfriend, and "Sin Wagon," which makes references to ammunition.

"Goodbye Earl" was not written by the Chicks, but the story line is similar to a real-life murder that took place in Tennessee in 1999. In that high-profile case, a woman was charged with murdering her deputy-sheriff husband with the help of her girlfriend.

The concern over "Sin Wagon," which was written by Natalie, Emily, and former Memphis songwriter Stephony Smith, focused on the student murders at Columbine High School. Would fans think the women advocated using violence to settle old scores? Record executives were concerned enough to bump the song from being the first release.

Martie hasn't backed away from the controversy. She and her band sisters stood up to the record label, and she's proud of their pluck. "They had three strong-headed blondes saying, 'Hey, it's on there,'" she told *Newsweek.* "And we know how to work it. We were playing 'Earl' live and telling the fans 'This'll be on the album.'"

Perhaps in response to Sony's legal department, the Chicks attempted to avoid controversy over the songs by putting a disclaimer in the album notes. While they didn't approve of murder, said the bizarre disclaimer, they did like to get even.

Initial reviews were encouraging. One of the first was in the *Tennessean:* "Cumulatively, the songs verify what we suspected about the trio following their monstrously successful *Wide Open Spaces* album: The Chicks are for real."

People magazine said the new album was "as full of down-home Texas twang as their first" and was "neither pop nor corn, just deep-fried country with lots of snap."

Also heaping praise on the new album was *Time* magazine. "The album's best cuts offer prime, primal, high-altitude country," said the reviewer. "Listeners should fly up to meet it."

Apparently, many did. The first week of its release, *Fly* sold an astonishing 341,000 copies, enough to propel it to Number One on *Billboard*'s Top 200 pop chart.

Even as they promoted their new album, the Dixie Chicks continued to receive accolades for *Wide Open Spaces*. At the thirty-third annual Country Music Association awards, held on September 22, 1999, in Nashville, the Dixie Chicks were given three major awards: top vocal group, top single, and video of the year. Accepting the video award was Thom Oliphant, the talented Nashville director who had made the Chicks come to life in his video of the single "Wide Open Spaces."

The Dixie Chicks opened the show that night with a performance of "Ready to Run," from their new album, *Fly*. It was an elaborately staged performance presented in a fairy-tale set that featured plenty of smoke, dancers, and airborne Peter Pans flying back and forth across the stage. The Dixie Chicks made their entrance by suddenly appearing from beneath gigantic hoop skirts.

While accepting one of the awards, Martie misspoke in true Chick fashion and said that their manager Simon Renshaw was not there because he was at home with "ammonia." Without missing a beat, Emily apologized for her sister, saying she had just had her hair dyed blonde again.

Noticeably absent that night from the group photographs was Martie's husband, Ted. Was he stashed away backstage somewhere, away from the prying eyes of the press? Or was he at home, baby-sitting his son?

"Ted knows how important things like that are to Martie," said a longtime friend. "If he wasn't there, that's really bad news."

As it turned out, Ted's absence at the Country Music Association awards was indeed bad news. On September 21, 1999, the day before the televised CMA awards ceremony took place, Martie and Ted separated. Ted took his son and went to their Woodstone Street address in Dallas, while Martie remained in their Nashville home.

On November 5, the divorce sought by Natalie was finalized. Under the terms of the final decree, Natalie agreed to pay Michael $25,000 in cash, followed by "rehabilitative alimony" of $225,000, payable in three annual installments of $75,000 each. Michael's interest in the house was assigned to Natalie, but Michael was allowed to keep "one bed and matching mattress selected by Wife," a dining room table, a purple chair and matching ottoman, a red end table and a green coffee table, and a home computer with desk and chair. Michael kept their 1997 Nissan Sentra; Natalie kept their 1999 Lexus. In addition, the divorce decree ordered that Natalie "not make derogatory statements about Husband or any statements that interfere with Husband's obtaining jobs or contracts." Michael agreed to do the same.

The most unusual requirement of the divorce decree was the stipulation that Michael tell Natalie "in person" that one of the reasons they moved to Nashville was so that he could obtain a job with a band. Apparently, Natalie was less concerned about paying her ex-husband alimony as she was in receiving what she considered an apology.

On November 19, two weeks after Natalie's divorce was finalized, Martie filed for divorce in a Nashville court, citing irreconcilable differences. The divorce petition stated that the couple anticipated entering into a marital dissolution agreement, an indication that Ted would not fight the divorce.

In early February 2000, the divorce was finalized. Under the terms of the agreement, Ted received $320,000 in cash, ownership of their home in Dallas, and their new Chevrolet Tahoe. Martie walked with her Nashville home, her Mercedes C280, and her freedom.

In addition to Martie's marital problems, there was concern among everyone associated with the group over Natalie's obvious weight gain, estimated by some to be in excess of thirty pounds. She looked huge at the CMA awards. Was it a temporary fluctuation, or was it a harbinger of worse things to come?

Overweight women have had successful careers in pop, jazz, and blues music—Mama Cass was the heart and soul of the Mamas and the Papas, and Ella Fitzgerald was never a waif—but seldom has that been the case in country music, where more rigid standards and more ingrained stereotypes apply.

If Natalie continued to gain weight, it probably would have no effect on her voice, aside from giving her a more breathy delivery, but it could be disastrous to a group that has marketed its sex appeal as a key ingredient to its success. "Mama and the Dixie Chicks" just doesn't have the same ring to it.

Music purists don't like to hear that appearance has eclipsed music in the selling of today's recording artists, but for confirmation that it is true, one need look no further than the plumpish Aretha Franklin. If hit albums were only about music, Aretha would be at the top of the charts, not Mariah Carey and Christina Aguilera.

As the Dixie Chicks looked forward to the year 2000, they did so with two chart-busting albums on the charts. *Wide Open Spaces* was the tenth best-selling pop album of 1999 and the second best-selling country album. The third best-selling country album of the year was *Fly*, with sales of over 2.6 million.

Their plans were to finish up their 1999 appearances in Australia before Christmas, then take five or six months off to rest and perhaps write songs for a new album before they kicked off their world tour in May or June 2000.

"We're going to take time off, because we're sick of the Chicks, and we don't want people to get sick of it," Natalie told *Rolling Stone* magazine. "We are going to give the album a chance to breathe without all the hype, and we need time to gather ourselves and to be human. I'm thinking of dying my hair black or getting extensions so I can be incognito for a while."

All that was true, as far as it went, but unspoken was the larger truth—that Martie and Natalie needed time to emotionally regroup after their divorces, and Natalie needed help slimming down before the group's next tour.

Early in 2000, nominations for the Forty-Second annual Grammy awards were announced. The Dixie Chicks were nominated in four categories, including "album of the year" and "country album." Ironically, one of their competitors in the "country album" category was Asleep at the Wheel's *Ride with Bob*, which also contained a song performed by the Chicks. There were, in effect, competing with themselves.

A week prior to the award ceremony, the Dixie Chicks came out of seclusion to perform on *The Tonight Show with Jay Leno*. Visually, the group had changed significantly since their last public performance. Emily had died her hair jet black, and Natalie looked as if she were still gaining weight. After their performance, they sat down with Leno for a brief conversation. He congratulated them on their four Grammy nominations, only to be corrected by Martie who declared they had *five* nominations.

Natalie said that the group would perform its next single, "Goodbye Earl," at the Grammys. Sounding defensive about the controversial song, Natalie told the audience that it was a "funny" tune, not a violent one as everyone seemed to think.

When they performed "Goodbye Earl" at the 2000 Grammys and introduced the video starring *NYPD Blue*'s Dennis Franz and *Ally McBeal*'s Jane Krakowski, the audience did not laugh at the "funny" song, but neither were there signs of outrage among the guests. Not until the song hit the radio airwaves were there signs of trouble. About twenty of 149 country stations polled by *Radio & Records* reported that they were not playing it. One indignant program director said, "What do we do a song about next: school shootings?"

That night, as the Dixie Chicks rushed on stage to accept the Grammy for "Best Country Album," Martie was suddenly overcome with emotion. With Emily looking on in visible discomfort, Martie grabbed the microphone and said that her personal life had taken a "beating" in 1999. "I just want to say to Ted and Carter," she continued, her eyes welling with tears, "I will always love you."

With the millennium dawning on a new age of country music, the troubled but ebullient Chicks sent out a message to their restless fans: See ya' in the summer!

At a 1999 Dixie Chicks concert in El Paso, Texas, Laura arrived with her daughter, Asia (who would celebrate her eighteenth birthday later in the year), and eight of her friends. When Laura asked Asia what she wanted for her birthday, she said that what she wanted most of all was to meet the Dixie Chicks. Laura made a few calls and obtained tickets to the concert, then arranged to take Asia and her friends backstage before the show.

Laura had not seen the newly-formed group perform live since 1995. She was shocked at what she saw. Where Emily once sought refuge in her shyness, she now aggressively danced with her arms up over her head, shimmying and shaking to the beat of the music. Shy Emmie had become a party animal.

"It used to be Martie who was the more outgoing," Laura relates. "Now it's Emily. She used to hide behind her banjo. Now she's doing this . . ." To demonstrate, Laura makes a dancing gesture with her arms up over her head. Way cool!

Before the concert, Laura took Asia and her friends backstage.

"Martie and Emily, already knowing me, recognized me and said, 'Oh, my gosh, it's so good seeing you. You're so grown up now,'" says Asia. "I had never met Natalie, and she was very sweet and she was like, nice to meet you, and everyone was real sweet and polite, and we had a fun time. We took them hair clips, and they liked them. Natalie wore hers out on stage, which I thought was neat."

To Natalie, Asia said, "I just want you to know I am your biggest fan!"

Natalie flashed that mischievous smile of hers, and said, "Does your mother know that?"

Asia nodded.

"I had no idea what to expect of Natalie," said Asia. "I had seen her picture and that was it. I didn't think she would be rude because Martie and Emily are so sweet. I didn't think they would have picked a grouch to be a Dixie Chick."

The Dixie Chicks of today bear little resemblance to the band Asia grew up with. "They're so hip looking and streamline and rocking," she says. "Before, they were just like a little homegrown band. In the beginning, I wasn't really a country music fan. It's only recently that I've started liking country music. I thought my mom was a little bit different. I thought of the Dixie Chicks as a group of girls hanging out, playing music, having fun. I didn't think they were trying to make it big. It was a little girls' club, and they dressed funny, wore sequins, and went around yodeling."

After the El Paso concert, Laura and Asia returned to their hotel. As it turned out, the Chicks were staying at the same hotel. Later that evening, they all met again downstairs in the lobby. Asia recalls them talking mostly about Emily's upcoming marriage to Charlie Robison. After talking for a while, Martie took them outside to see their new tour bus.

"It's awesome," says Asia of the bright red vehicle, which has no special markings on the outside. "I'm sure it's less cool when you have to live in it twenty-four/seven, but it seemed so luxurious, compared to what they used to have to ride in."

When you first step into the bus, you enter a small living room, then beyond that, a miniature kitchen with a small stand-up bar (there are no bar stools). The carpet throughout is navy blue, and the walls are covered with wood trim. At the rear of the bus, where the stars customarily have the master bedroom, the Chicks have what could best be described as a den. It contains a couch, and it is where the women watch television, view tapes on a VCR, and listen to music.

What impressed Asia the most were the sleeping arrangements. Between the kitchen and the den, the walls narrow into a hallway that contains a triple layer of bunk beds constructed so that they appear to have been built into the wall. In true Chick fashion, the women designed the sleeping arrangements so that one woman did not receive preferential treatment over the others. If there was one thing Martie and Emily had learned on the road, it was that democracy was essential to living together in close quarters.

Martie showed Asia where she slept: in the middle bunk, between Emily and Natalie. On the bed were Martie's cell phone and a pile of magazines. "They were very skinny single beds," recalls Asia. "They were skinnier than the beds they have on trains. It reminded me of a bed I once had at camp."

Asia left with stars in her eyes: "It was my most memorable day."

The experience also gave Asia a new understanding of what her mother was thinking and feeling all those years. "When she left the band, when it ended, I felt sad for her because she had really worked at it," says Asia. "When they got Natalie, I was, like, 'Mom, you're like that other Beatle, you know the drummer they had before Ringo Starr.' Nobody knows who he is because he was there before Ringo Star. Everyone knows there was another Dixie Chick, but they don't know who she is and where she is now."

Since she "left" the band, Laura has packed away all her dreams of making it big in music, but she has not stopped singing. "She still sings all the time," says Asia, breaking into laughter. "For a daughter to hear her mom sing all the time, sometimes that can drive a person wild. If your mom sang around the house all the time, wouldn't that sort of drive you nuts? She'll be singing, and I'll say, 'Don't sing, let's talk.'"

Laura, who listens to an inner voice, one that keeps her on course in good times and bad, could no more stop singing than she could stop breathing. In her own way, she is still singing harmony with the Dixie Chicks, if only from a distance.

Once a Chick, always a Chick.

"I'm so happy for them," says Laura. "I will always love that band and will forever support them. We had ups and downs, but we did it together, holding hands."

Laura laughs, her eyes dancing around her thoughts. "That's another girl thing. When the shit hits the fan, we hold hands." She thinks about that a minute and then shakes her head. "Guys never do that."

DISCOGRAPHY

ALBUMS

■ 1991
Thank Heavens for Dale Evans
Crystal Clear Sound
PRODUCERS: the Dixie Chicks
SONGS: "The Cowboy Lives Forever,"
"I Want to be a Cowboy's
Sweetheart," "Thunderheads,"
"Long Roads," "Who Will Be the
Next One," "Brilliancy," "Thank
Heavens for Dale Evans," "This
Heart of Mine," "Storm Out on the
Sea," "West Texas Wind," "Rider,"
"Green River," "Salty," and "Bring
It on Home to Me."

■ 1992
Little Ol' Cowgirl
Crystal Clear Sound
PRODUCERS: Larry Seyer and the Dixie
Chicks
SONGS: "Little Ol' Cowgirl," "A Road
Is Just a Road," "She'll Find Better
Things to Do," "Irish Medley,"
"You Send Me," "Just a Bit Like
Me," "A Heart That Can," "Past the
Point of Rescue," "Beatin' Around
the Bush," "Two of a Kind,"
"Standin' by the Bedside," "Aunt
Mattie's Quilt," "Hallelujah, I Just

Love Him So," and "Pink
Toenails."

■ 1993
Shouldn't a Told You That
Crystal Clear Sound
PRODUCER: Steve Fishell
SONGS: "Whistles and Bells," "I'm
Falling Again," "Shouldn't a Told
You That," "Planet of Love,"
"Desire," "There Goes My Dream,"
"One Heart Away," "The Thrill Is in
the Chase," "I Wasn't Looking for
You," and "I've Only Got Myself to
Blame."

■ 1998
Wide Open Spaces
Monument Records
PRODUCERS: Paul Worley and Blake
Chancey
SONGS: "I Can Love You Better," "Wide
Open Spaces," "Loving Arms,"
"There's Your Trouble," "You Were
Mine," "Never Say Die," "Tonight
the Heartache's on Me," "Let 'er
Rip," "Once You've Loved
Somebody," "I'll Take Care of You,"
"Am I the Only One (Who's Ever
Felt This Way)," and "Give It Up Or
Let Me Go."

■ 1999
Fly
Monument Records
PRODUCERS: Blake Chancey and Paul Worley
SONGS: "Ready to Run," "If I Fall, You're Goin' Down with Me," "Cowboy Take Me Away," "Cold Day in July," "Goodbye Earl," "Hello Mr. Heartache," "Don't Waste Your Heart," "Sin Wagon," "Without You," "Some Days You Gotta Dance," "Hole in My Head," "Heartbreak Town," and "Let Him Fly."

SINGLES

■ 1991
"Home on the Radar Range" ("Christmas Swing" / "The Flip Side")
PRODUCERS: the Dixie Chicks and Larry Seyer
SONGWRITERS: "Christmas Swing," the Dixie Chicks and friends; "The Flip Side," Robin Lynn Macy, Lisa Brandenburg, Laura Lynch

■ 1998
"I Can Love You Better"
SONGWRITERS: Kostas and Pamela Brown Hayes
CD: *Wide Open Spaces*

■ 1998
"There's Your Trouble"
SONGWRITERS: Tia Sillers and Mark Selby
CD: *Wide Open Spaces*

■ 1998
"Wide Open Spaces"
SONGWRITER: Susan Gibson
CD: *Wide Open Spaces*

■ 1998
"You Were Mine"
SONGWRITERS: Emily Erwin and Martie Seidel
CD: *Wide Open Spaces*

■ 1999
"Ready to Run"
SONGWRITERS: Martie Seidel and Marcus Hummon
CD: *Fly*

■ 1999
"Cowboy Take Me Away"
SONGWRITERS: Martie Seidel and Marcus Hummon
CD: *Fly*

■ 2000
"Goodbye Earl"
SONGWRITER: Dennis Linde
CD: *Fly*

VIDEOS

■ 1998
"I Can Love You Better"
DIRECTOR: Amos/Kennedy
CD: *Wide Open Spaces*

■ 1998
"There's Your Trouble"
DIRECTOR: Thom Oliphant
PRODUCER: David Pritchart
CD: *Wide Open Spaces*

■ 1998
"Wide Open Spaces"
DIRECTOR: Thom Oliphant
PRODUCER: David Pritchart
CD: *Wide Open Spaces*

■ 1998
"You Were Mine"
DIRECTOR: Adolfo Doring

PRODUCER: Jaye Nydick
CD: *Wide Open Spaces*

■ 1999
"Ready to Run"
DIRECTOR: Evan Bernard
PRODUCER: Paul Albanese
CD: *Fly*

■ 1999
"Cowboy Take Me Away"
DIRECTOR: Nancy Bardawil
CD: *Fly*

■ 2000
"Goodbye Earl"
DIRECTOR: Keeley Gould
CD: *Fly*

AWARDS

■ 1991
Dallas Observer
"Best Country and Western Band of the Year"

■ 1998
Country Music Association
"Horizon Award" and "Group of the Year"

■ 1999
American Music Awards
    "Favorite New Country Artist"
Grammy Awards
    "Best Performance by a Country Duo or Group" and "Best Country Album"

Academy of Country Music Awards
    "Album of the Year," "Top New Vocal Duet or Group," and "Top Duet or Group."
TNN Music City News Country Awards
    "Female Star of Tomorrow" and "Vocal Band of the Year"
Country Music Association
    "Best Video"
    "Group of the Year"
    "Single of the Year"

■ 2000
Grammy Awards
"Best Country Album" and "Best Performance by a Country Duo or Group"

RECOMMENDED WEB SITES

Academy of Country Music
 www.acmcountry.com
Robert Brooks
 dixiechicks.mixedsignal.net/
Country Music Association
 www.countrymusic.org
Cyber Country Magazine
 www.cyber-country.com
Whitney Israel
 www.geocities.com/nashville/opry/
 5727

KYNG radio of Dallas–Fort Worth
 www.superstarcountry.com
Nici Larson
 www.geocities.com/Nashville/9426/
 chicks.html
Nashville Network and Country Music
 Television
 www.country.com
Sony Records / Nashville
 www.sonynashville.com/

BIBLIOGRAPHY

AUTHOR INTERVIEWS

Asia Abraham (1999)
Cary Banks (1999)
Roy Bode (1999)
Robert Brooks (1999)
Leigh Browning (1999)
Al Cooley (1999)
RuNell Coons (1999)
Ben Dixon (1999)
Sarah Godcher (1999)
Janelle Hackenbeck (1999)
Sara Hickman (1994)
Whitney Israel (1999)
Stephen John (1999)
Nici Larson (1999)
DeAnna Lee (1999)
Angie McIsaac (1999)

Ken Michaels (1999 e-mail)
Abra Moore (1997)
Greg Morrow (1999)
Vicki Nash (1999)
Thom Oliphant (1999)
Katie Pruett (1999)
Randy Ricks (1999)
Jay Rury (1999)
Tom Van Schaik (1999)
Larry Seyer (1999)
David Skepner (1999)
Michael Sommermeyer (1999)
Danielle Syx (1999)
Johnny Thorn (1999)
Laura Lynch Tull (1999)
Cynthia Wagner (1999)

BOOKS

Dickerson, James. *Women On Top: The Quiet Revolution That's Rocking the American Music Industry.* New York: Billboard Books, 1998.

Moses, Robert, Alicia Potter and Beth Rowen, editors. *A&E Entertainment Almanac.* Boston and New York: Houghton Mifflin Company, 1996.

Oermann, Robert K., and Mary A. Burwack. *Finding Her Voice: The Saga of Women in Country Music.* New York: Crown Publishers, 1993.

MAGAZINE AND NEWSPAPER ARTICLES

Adels, Robert. "Talent Review: Dixie Chicks." *Cash Box,* September 5, 1992.

Bandy, Julie. "Ladies lead the way as sales soar." *Country Weekly,* March 2, 1999.

Brodie, Honor, Monica Corcoran, Robin Sayers, and Heidi Sherma. "Dixie Chicks." *In Style,* July 1999.

Boucher, Geoff. "Hill Makes History With 5 Wins." *Los Angeles Times,* February 25, 1999.

Brunner, Rob, and Laura Morgan. "Tour Guide," *Entertainment Weekly,* July 16, 1999.

Catlin, Roger. "Music first, gender second." *The Hartford Courant,* August 1, 1997.

Clark, Renee. "Can the Dixie Chicks Make It in the Big Time?" *Dallas Life,* March 1, 1992.

Crain, Zac. "Teaching a (history) lesson." *Dallas Observer,* December 10, 1998.

"Fashion Police." *US,* July 1999.

Gates, David, and Devin Gordon. "Good Old Grrrls." *Newsweek,* September 27, 1999.

Helligar, Jeremy and Chris Rose. "Feather Friends." *People,* September 28, 1998.

Herman, James Patrick. "The Last of Lilith." *Elle,* July 1999.

Hess, Christopher. "Texas Platters." *Austin Chronicle,* vol. 17/issue 32.

Hitts, Roger. "Dixie Chick's hush-hush wedding." *Star,* May 18, 1999.

Hitts, Roger. "Dixie Split: Chicks Set to Call it Quits." *Star,* February 23, 1998.

Holden, Larry. "Ruling the Country Roost," *Country Weekly,* July 6, 1999.

Hoops, Jana. "Dixie Chicks Put Upbeat Fun Into Country." *The Clarion-Ledger,* December 31, 1998.

Jamison, Laura. "They're Not Just Whistling Dixie." *Seventeen,* April 1999.

Jinkins, Shirley. "Chicks Still Click." *Fort Worth Star-Telegram,* August 30, 1991.

Ladouceur, Liisa. "Sarah McLachlan." *Pulse,* July 1997.

McCall, Michael. "It's a Chick Thing." *Los Angeles Times,* November 22, 1998.

Myerson, Allen. "Big D's Unofficial Index of Economic Health." *The New York Times,* September 12, 1994.

Nichols, Lee. "Lloyd Maines: The Guy Is Everywhere." *Austin Chronicle,* vol. 16/issue 10.

Noles, Tammy. "The Dixie Chicks." *Trendsetter,* January 1993.

Orr, Charlene. "Continental Drift." *Billboard,* June 4, 1994.

Pareles, Jon. "Forget the Hard Rock: It's Support for Sisterhood." *The New York Times,* July 7, 1997.

Pollack, Marc. "Hill has handful with five trophies as ladies sparkle." *Hollywood Reporter,* February 25, 1999.

Richmond, Ray. "The 41st Annual Grammy Awards." *Daily Variety,* February 25, 1999.

Rutkoski, Rex. "Dixie Chicks: The Only New Success Story of '98." *Shania Twain and the Country Girl Explosion,* May 1999.

Shuster, Fred. "Do Blondes Have More Fun?" *Daily News,* November 11, 1998.

Skanse, Richard. "Hot Chicks." *Rolling Stone,* October 28, 1999.

Spencer, Amy. "Chicks Appeal." *TV Guide,* January 9, 1999.

Tarnow, Noah. "Dixie Chicks." *Rolling Stone,* December 10, 1998.

Wictor, Thomas. "Unsung Bass Stylists." *Bass Player,* April 1997.

Wilonsky, Robert. "Nashville Women." *Dallas Observer,* March 12, 1998.

COURT DOCUMENTS

Robin Macy vs. Martie Erwin, Emily Erwin and Laura Lynch and the Dixie Chicks. Number 94-01489-M, District Court of Dallas County, Texas, 28th Judicial District (1992–94).
Natalie Maines Tarabay vs. Michael Victor Tarabay. File number 99D96, Fourth Circuit, 20th Judicial District, Nashville, Tennessee (1999).
Martha Eleanor Seidel vs. Ted Ashley Seidel. File number 99D3125, Fourth Circuit, 20th Judicial District, Nashville, Tennessee (1999).

SONY RECORDS PRESS RELEASES

February 4, 1998. "Dixie Chicks Make Dazzling Debut." Sony Music Nashville.
March 18, 1998. "'Wide Open Spaces' Fastest Rising Debut Disc by a Country Group in History of SoundScan." Sony Music Nashville.
June 19, 1998. "Dixie Chicks Strike Gold." Sony Music Nashville.
July 28, 1998. "Dixie Chicks: 'There's Your Trouble.'" Sony Music Nashville.
October 21, 1998. "Dixie Chicks Score Top 10 Album." Sony Music Nashville.
December 8, 1998. "Country's Hottest Act Hit Triple Platinum With 'Wide Open Spaces.'" Sony Music Nashville.
January 5, 1999. "Dixie Chicks Grab Three Grammy Nominations." Sony Music Nashville.
January 21, 1999. "Dixie Chicks 'Wide Open Spaces' Biggest Selling Country Album in the Nation." Sony Music Nashville.
February 2, 1999. "Four Million and Counting." Sony Music Nashville.
April 27, 1999. "Dixie Chicks to Co-Headline Lilith Fair With Sarah McLachlan, Sheryl Crow." Sony Music Nashville.
June 6, 1999. "Group Sells Over Six Million Copies of 'Wide Open Spaces.'" Sony Music Nashville.

ABOUT THE AUTHOR

Award-winning author James L. Dickerson has written extensively about the music industry. The former editor and publisher of *Nine-O-One Network,* at one time the third largest circulation music magazine in the country, he also served as the executive producer of *Pulsebeat—The Voice of the Heartland,* a country music syndication that was aired by nearly 100 radio stations from coast to coast in the late 1980s.

Two of Dickerson's music books, *Goin' Back to Memphis* (1996) and *That's Alright, Elvis* (1997), which he cowrote with Scotty Moore, have been nominated for the prestigious Ralph J. Gleason Award, presented annually by BMI, New York University, and *Rolling Stone* magazine to the top music books of the year.

Dickerson resides in Nashville, Tennessee.

INDEX